YOU
ARE
Amazing

YOU ARE AMAZING

Text by Caroline Roope

An Hachette UK Company
www.hachette.co.uk

Vie Books, an imprint of Summersdale Publishers Ltd
Part of Octopus Publishing Group Limited
Carmelite House
50 Victoria Embankment
LONDON
EC4Y 0DZ
UK

www.summersdale.com

Printed and bound in China

ISBN: 978-1-83799-168-6

Substantial discounts on bulk quantities of Summersdale books are available to corporations, professional associations and other organizations. For details contact general enquiries: telephone: +44 (0) 1243 771107 or email: enquiries@summersdale.com.

Disclaimer
Neither the author nor the publisher can be held responsible for any injury, loss or claim – be it health, financial or otherwise – arising out of the use, or misuse, of the suggestions made herein. This book is not intended as a substitute for the medical advice of a doctor or physician. If you are experiencing problems with your physical or mental health, it is always best to follow the advice of a medical professional.

YOU
ARE
Amazing

A FEEL-GOOD GUIDE
TO HELP YOU LOVE YOUR
MIND, BODY AND LIFE

CONTENTS

WELCOME

Welcome to *You Are Amazing*, a book that will help you celebrate how fabulous you are.

If you're feeling a bit low, having a difficult day, or just generally feeling a bit *bleurgh*, it's easy to forget how incredible you really are. Self-doubt creeps in, your confidence takes a knock and before you know it, you've managed to convince yourself that you're insignificant and living an unremarkable life. And then – annoyingly – that becomes your normal.

But what if you could wake up every day knowing you're fabulous and you're going to achieve incredible things? That would be brilliant, wouldn't it?

When we believe in ourselves, anything is possible – so it makes sense that if we work on our self-belief, we can stop thinking that we're average and start recognizing that we're amazing.

And that's where this book will help. It's packed full of tips, activities and general awesomeness to start empowering you to feel better about yourself.

So, dip in and get ready to start living your best life – because you are amazing!

What this book will do for you

This book will inspire you to start loving yourself – "flaws" and all – both inside and out. You don't have to be perfect to be amazing (not even a tiny bit), but you do need a little self-belief and a positive attitude.

This book will equip you with exactly that, so you can start recognizing and celebrating your fabulousness.

It'll take you on a journey of self-discovery: ever wondered how your brain processes your thoughts and turns them into emotions? Or what type of thinker you are? Look no further!

This book will also enable you to love your body – no matter how you think you look, or what you think other people think about how you look.

And crucially, it'll help you learn how to love your life – because we all deserve to live our best life.

There's amazingness inside every one of us – sometimes we just need a nudge in the right direction and some guidance to help coax it out. But know this – the more we begin to understand ourselves, the easier it becomes to start realizing and accepting just how amazing we really are.

Your journey starts here. You've got this!

How to use this book

This book is for you if...

◆ You put yourself under pressure to be "perfect".

◆ You compare yourself and your situation unfavourably to others.

◆ You seek validation from the people around you and change yourself to "fit in".

◆ You find it difficult to silence your inner critic.

◆ You tend to focus on your "flaws".

◆ You struggle with body image.

◆ You over-analyze and dwell on negative experiences.

◆ You feel like you're not good enough and put yourself down.

◆ You're sensitive to criticism or negative feedback.

If this sounds like you sometimes – or even all the time – then this book is designed to help. It aims to help you see positive long-term change in your mindset, which isn't focused on outside perceptions of "success". Being amazing isn't about securing that promotion, or passing an exam, or being the perfect parent. The reality is, you don't have to achieve amazing things to be amazing – because being amazing comes from within.

It's having the resilience to give every day your best shot and knowing your worth. Or it could simply be knowing who you are, and having the courage to live the life you want to live. You can do all of this. Why? Because you are amazing!

PART ONE:
Love your mind

You don't need to be a doctor or a scientist to know that the brain is an amazing piece of evolutionary equipment. Did you know that there are approximately 86 billion neurons in a human brain of average size, all firing and receiving signals that help us to think, act and breathe? In fact, our brains are so amazing that they're mostly still a mystery – scientists are still trying to work out just what they're capable of. But one thing we can be sure of is that if we look after our brain, it'll look after us. Read on to discover how you can boost your brain, give it all the good feels, and, most importantly, how you can learn to love it.

Your brilliant brain

Everything we do, for the duration of our lives, is controlled by our brain.

Let's just let that sink in for a second...

Pretty amazing, right? Our brain is literally the control centre for our entire being, thinking, learning, breathing, walking, talking, blinking, scratching, hearing, seeing... you get the picture. It's also remarkable that with all that going on, it only weighs about as much as a cauliflower and looks like a large walnut. Yet despite its slightly odd appearance, it's also responsible for moments of greatness – from falling in love to saving someone's life, as well as making a loved one laugh, learning a new skill and all those mini lightbulb* moments when something fantastic occurs to us.

We couldn't do anything without our brains, so it's extra-important that we keep them healthy by flexing our brainy muscles regularly. Because when things get tough, it's your brain that's going to get you out of trouble. Fact.

Later in this section, you'll find some brain-boosting activities, as well as tips and techniques to calm your mind and train your brain to cope with negativity. But most importantly, we'll be showing a ton of appreciation for the big walnut in your head and all the fabulous things it allows you to do – like reading this book!

---

* Incidentally, science has proven that the brain runs continuously on only 12 watts of power. That's roughly the same as a low-wattage light bulb!

Your personal self-storage facility

Neuroscientists recently discovered that the human brain may be able to hold the same amount of information in its memory as the entire internet – even though it only uses the same amount of electricity needed to power a dim lightbulb (see page 12). Just to put that into perspective, to run a computer with the same memory and processing power would require one gigawatt (one billion watts) of power. You'd need an entire nuclear power station for that one computer, whereas our brain "computer" can do the same with just 20 watts.

This may be difficult to believe when you can't even remember what you ate for breakfast or what time your Pilates class starts, but memory matters – and here's why. Not only is memory important for knowledge and being able to recall that knowledge in any given situation (for instance, knowing how to drive a car or read a map), but it also informs our thoughts and helps us to create our world view. Our understanding of the world around us is built on the information we store from previous experiences – information that resides in our memory. Plus, research has shown that the more we exercise our memory by filling it with knowledge, the more we can increase our capacity to learn.

So, what's the takeaway from all this? Your brain is like a limitless self-storage facility that is always hungry for more knowledge to keep it healthy – so just keep filling it up! Anything that helps to make new connections in your brain will be helping to keep your memory mighty.

THE POWER OF THREE

Apart from generally being fabulous, your brain has three main functions:

1. Managing your unconscious or "automatic" functions. Your heartbeat, breathing, digestion, blinking, swallowing and body temperature are all examples of "automatic" functions. Essentially, the things that keep us alive.

2. Managing your conscious or "motor" functions. For instance, movements such as walking or running, gesturing with our hands and face, balance, posture and speech.

3. Thinking, emotions, behaviour and all our senses: sight, sound, smell, touch and taste.

So, as well as powering our body with automatic functions (which we're often not even aware of) and giving us the ability to do all the things we need to do to live our daily lives, it also allows us to experience a range of emotions. These feelings are generated in a part of your brain called the temporal lobe.

Whether you're feeling happy, sad, joyful, disappointed, grateful, upset, loved or optimistic, it's your emotions and thoughts that make you... well, you.

So, what exactly is a "thought"?

Buckle up folks because we're about to go deep. The simplest definition for a "thought" might go something like this: words that appear in our brain, that only we think, that cause us to do something.

An example of a thought might be: "I don't want to get out of bed today." But did the thought just spontaneously pop into your head? Or did something else trigger it? Is it just the physical response of your brain to an outside stimulus (such as an alarm clock, which causes a reaction – in this case, the knowledge that time is passing) or is it a manifestation of something deeper within your soul? Science tells us that thoughts can be explained by chemical changes in the brain, but some philosophers believed that the mind is separate from the body, and therefore thoughts are unconnected to the body too. (Deep stuff.)

If we take science as our starting point, we know that whenever we have a thought, there is a corresponding chemical reaction in our mind and body. That means that what we think can affect how we feel. And if what we think changes how we feel, it makes sense to try to harness that mental power to do ourselves some good. It could be as simple as switching up your mindset: "I love getting out of bed and starting a new day." And the great news is, we can apply this to other areas of our lives too and start nurturing a more positive outlook.

> When you change your thinking, you are also having a positive impact on your mind and your body.

What type of thinker are you?

We're all utterly unique, so it makes sense that we all have brains that think in diverse ways.

If you want to discover which type of thinker you are, take this light-hearted quiz to find out.

If you're writing a shopping list, you...

A) Order it by where the items are in the shop

B) Consult the rest of your household as you write the list

C) Consult your weekly meal plan and then write what you need on the list

D) Don't bother with a list. You'll buy whatever takes your fancy

If you're teaching someone how to use a new gadget or piece of equipment, you...

A) Break it down into lots of steps

B) Relate it to something that is already familiar to them

C) Give them the gist of it and then let them try it on their own

D) Explain all the information that you've memorized, and write them a personalized set of instructions

After watching a film with a friend, what's the first topic of discussion?

A) The plot and how it unfolded

B) What you liked or disliked about the film

C) Whether you guessed the plot twist before the end

D) The aesthetics of the production, such as the clothes, special effects, location and set

When you're out for dinner with friends or family, you...

A) Quietly listen to everybody else until somebody speaks to you

B) Join in a conversation that has already started

C) Go around the table making sure you speak to everyone individually

D) Engage everyone in a lively debate or game

What was your favourite subject at school?

A) Maths and/or science

B) English and/or drama

C) Woodwork, textiles, or food technology

D) Art and design

If you're planning a holiday, you...

A) Read lots of guidebooks and consult maps so you can get the idea of an itinerary

B) Take recommendations from websites, magazines or friends

C) Prepare a full itinerary before you go, and book meals and attractions before leaving

D) Rock up at your destination and see what happens!

What sort of holiday destination appeals to you the most?

A) City breaks with loads of cultural attractions

B) Cruises, adventure, nightlife or scheduled activities

C) A themed holiday such as a cookery school or a writers' retreat

D) Anywhere unusual that's off the tourist trail and allows for exploration and "roughing it"

What do you value most in your close relationships?

A) Honesty and loyalty. Knowing you can always count on each other

B) Adventure and a love of trying new things together

C) Reliability. You'll always be there for each other no matter what life throws at you

D) Intelligence. You need to be stimulated mentally and have an intellectual connection

Mostly As

You're a logical thinker – your ideas are methodical, considered and realistic. To solve life's problems, you like to formulate a solution based on all the data you can gather and make rational decisions.

Mostly Bs

You're a collaborative thinker – you're happiest when you're letting everyone have a say. You take on board other people's ideas and suggestions to help you develop your own ideas to tackle a challenge.

Mostly Cs

You're a practical thinker – you like to plan meticulously in life and are usually the most organized in a group of people. When faced with a challenge, you use tried-and-tested strategies to fix it and will often evaluate your performance as you go. You're most comfortable when you're anticipating how the problem will unfold before it has a chance to happen.

Mostly Ds

You're an abstract thinker – you're creative and playful in your approach to life, and you're often the one doing the "blue sky thinking" and coming up with big, original ideas. You're unfazed by a challenge and like to solve it using gut feeling and instincts, alongside existing knowledge.

A mixture of As, Bs, Cs and Ds

You are an all-rounder who uses a flexible approach depending on the scenario. Some people have a defined way of thinking. You, however, just go with the flow!

Always end
the day with
a positive
thought;
tomorrow
is a fresh
opportunity
to make
things better

WHEN YOUR BRAIN HAS A BLIP

When a computer malfunctions, it'll often give us an error message – something like "Oops, something went wrong". As we've already seen, our brains are so amazing it's like carrying around our own personal computer in our head – albeit one that looks like a walnut. But the downside of this is that sometimes our brain likes to behave like a computer by generating what psychologists call "thinking errors". Just like the irritation of a computer that isn't behaving itself, our brains can also play havoc with our emotions.

Thinking errors are negative ways of thinking about yourself and the world around you. They sound utterly convincing, but often these thoughts just aren't real. They've been completely fabricated by your brain (thanks, Brain), and they're inaccurate and have no basis in fact.

Here are some common thinking errors and what they might sound like:

All-or-nothing thinking:
I'm a failure at life.

Over-generalizing: Something small goes wrong, so now life will go wrong.

Focusing on the negative: If one thing goes wrong, I can't move past the problem or stop thinking about it.

Fortune-telling: I know I'll fail and embarrass myself.

Catastrophizing: He didn't respond to my email. Something bad has happened.

Mind-reading: I know everyone thinks I'm stupid.

Magnified thinking: I forgot to get dinner. I'm the worst husband ever.

Unrealistic expectations: I must be perfect, all the time.

Negative comparison: She's prettier and more successful than me.

Blaming yourself: Everything goes wrong and it's all my fault.

Putting yourself down: I'm a terrible person.

Feelings are facts: I feel ugly, so I must be ugly. I acted like a jerk, so I am a jerk.

Blaming others: I would be a better person if people were nicer. It's your fault I'm so messed up.

Spinning the negative into a positive

One of the most effective ways to tackle negative thoughts is to develop your inner *spin doctor*. This means catching the negative thought before it takes hold and giving it a positive spin. Then all you need to do is listen to the positive narrative in your mind instead. A bit like this:

I'm stupid. → This is tricky, but I'll get there.

This is pointless. I'm going to fail. → I'll go one step at a time and try my best. It's OK to fail.

People think I'm an idiot. → They know I'm a beginner and need some support.

I messed that up. I'm useless. → I can learn from this and try again another way.

I never do anything right. → If I keep persevering, I'll know I tried my best.

SPIN IT YOURSELF

Now it's your turn. Next time your brain has a blip and a thinking error appears, write it here.

Can you put a positive spin on it? Take your time. You can always come back to it later if it's not helpful right now.

Glass half empty

When we're feeling low, it's difficult to feel optimistic about anything. We all know the old saying about perceiving the glass to be half empty.

Perhaps you've fallen out with a loved one, or you're having a tough time at work or college. At times like this, it's easy for negative thoughts (like the ones we've identified) to take hold and make you feel even worse. And before you know it, you're telling yourself you're useless at everything and completely undeserving of all the good things in life.

It sucks, but it *is* a totally normal function of a healthy brain. As humans we're blessed with the ability to experience emotional highs, such as love, joy, excitement, happiness and hope, but the trade-off is accepting that sometimes we'll have to experience some lows too. And that's OK. Embrace the low points; acknowledge the negativity and know that it'll pass. You'll have a greater appreciation of the highs when you emerge on the other side.

Glass half full

Positive thinking isn't just about burying those irritating negative thoughts or avoiding difficult emotions. There are some simple ideas you can incorporate into your life that'll help make a problem seem more manageable and help the glass look half full – hurrah! For instance, why not try hopeful journalling to help you visualize positive outcomes (see pages 40 and 41) or reviewing your life goals to see if you can break them down into some instantly achievable and positivity-boosting mini goals (see pages 156 and 157)? There are lots more half-full helpers in this book.

Is that thought useful? Or useless?

It's OK to have negative thoughts. They keep us safe: "I'm not great on the treadmill, so I'll have to go slow, or I'll go flying off and embarrass myself." They can also be quite useful for helping us achieve difficult things: "I'm gutted I failed that test and I'm disappointed in myself, so I'll be trying extra hard next time."

But unhelpful negative self-talk ("I'm useless", for example) can be a little bit sly. It seamlessly blends into all your other daily thoughts to the point where you don't even notice it's chattering away on repeat.

The trick is to develop a filter so you can identify why a specific thought is floating around your head at a particular time and separate the useful thoughts from the useless ones.

For instance, there may have been a trigger for the useless thought. If you're idly scrolling through social media and a celebrity influencer is showing off their new "bikini body" it might encourage you to compare yourself unfavourably. That would be a useless thought, so don't waste your time with it!

In a world full of messages that our minds are eager to absorb, we need to be able to differentiate between the messages that are worth listening to and those that aren't.

The only message your brain needs to soak up is this:

YOU ARE *Amazing*

Catch it, write it, bin it

Things you need:

- **Paper**
- **Pen**
- **Recycling bin or waste container**
- **A mind full of negative thoughts**

Do you get a satisfying feeling when you destroy something that's really getting on your nerves? Well, you can do that with your thoughts too. Physically disposing of the negative thoughts that are bringing you down can be a powerful way to realign your thinking.

But first you need a physical manifestation of your thoughts – which is where the pen and paper come in. So, scribble away! You're going to throw it away so don't hold back. Perhaps you've just got a few negative niggles to write down, or maybe this is your chance to exorcise something bigger.

The theory goes that if you create something that exists outside of yourself to represent these thoughts, such as drawings or words on the page, and then symbolically let these things go by destroying them, it can help release the negativity from your mind.

Cherish the good times

It's easy to let good moments slip away from us without truly reflecting on how amazing they've made us feel. Maybe a friend baked something for you and then surprised you with it – for no other reason than wanting to show their appreciation for you. Or perhaps you or your child achieved something that's worth celebrating, and you're practically bursting with pride. Holding on to the emotions we feel in positive moments, and then remembering later how they made us feel is brilliant for nurturing a long-lasting stream of positive thoughts and emotions.

Brain training 101

Want to hear something amazing? Our brain can change its make-up by using positive experiences to create feelings of happiness and contentment.

It's all to do with the neurons in your brain (the cells that transmit information) which is why neuroscientists say, "neurons that fire together, wire together."

Put simply, it means that passing mental states, such as happiness, joy, feeling loved, self-confidence and inner peace, can become neural traits that are embedded in the fabric of your brain.

If you experience more of these brain-changing emotions on a regular basis, it trains your brain to be happy and have a positive outlook. For example, if you want to feel more confident, build accomplishment into your life: set yourself some goals for your day and make sure you see them through. Or if you want to nurture compassion, simply practise more acts of kindness, such as checking up on a vulnerable neighbour, or paying someone a compliment. The process is the same as learning a new skill, the more we practise it, the more messages are passed along the neurons in our brain and the more connections are made.

Absorb the positive moments as you experience them and let the goodness grow in your mind. You'll be priming your memory to become more efficient at drawing on this positivity whenever you need a boost or if times get tough.

Affirmation lucky dip

Things you need:

- Paper
- Pen
- A jar or box
- A mind full of positive thoughts

This is kind of the reverse of what you've just done on page 27. Affirmations are short impactful statements that help us shift our mindset towards positivity. They encapsulate inspiring ideas and can help us change the way we think about ourselves.

Write each of the affirmations below on a small piece of paper and then put them in a jar or box. Every time you need a pick-me-up or you're facing a challenge, pull one out at random and repeat it to yourself – the idea being that the more you repeat a statement, the more you'll believe it. You can also add your own affirmations. This makes them personal to you and gives you ownership of them, which enhances their impact.

I do my best, and that is good enough

I can do this

I am amazing

I believe in myself

I am grateful to be me

I am enough

My voice deserves to be heard

I am resilient when facing a challenge

My mistakes help me to grow

I trust myself to make the right decisions

COPING WITH THE BIG STUFF

Adulting can sometimes make us feel a bit weary. There's always *something* that needs to be done – tidying the overflowing cupboard in the kitchen, starting that project you've been avoiding, making the kids packed lunches, helping your friend move into a new flat, spending the afternoon doing boring life admin – and so on ad infinitum.

The to-do list seems never-ending, and the monotony of life and all it entails starts to wear us down. Add in a dose of work or college-related stress, relationship issues, parenting anxieties or financial challenges and it can quickly become overwhelming – suddenly we're dealing with some big feelings and emotions that start to have a negative impact on our well-being.

It happens. It's life. But that doesn't mean we have to suffer our way through it. We can arm ourselves with a set of tools to manage those moments when the big feelings start to become a burden.

You could try meditation to help you clear out your brain clutter (see page 37) or mastering mindfulness and calming your emotions when they're starting to make you feel uncomfortable (see pages 42 and 43). There are lots of different exercises you can deploy when you're next dodging one of life's many curveballs.

Check in with yourself

Stop everything for a moment. Don't think about it – just stop.

How are you right now?

Before you answer with the standard "OK", try to tune in to yourself for a moment.

How are you *really*?

You might like to find somewhere comfortable and quiet, then close your eyes and take a deep breath. Can you identify any niggling feelings or emotions just below the surface? Consider the prompts across these pages – you can write your answers down or just think about them for a moment.

Checking in with yourself allows you to take stock of your feelings and understand why you're feeling them. This will help you to process and manage your emotions, as well as helping you to think about how you might change what you can control and deal with what you can't.

I feel...

_____

_____

_____

My energy levels are...

_____

_____

My emotions are...

_____

_____

My body feels...

_____

_____

My mind feels...

_____

_____

It would feel good to...

_____

_____

I'm thinking about...

_____

_____

_____

Name that feeling

As we're in the "feeling zone" right now, it's a good chance to think about how we frame what we're feeling inside. Studies have shown when you name what you're feeling, the feeling itself loses its impact and you become better able to control it. This is hugely helpful when you've got the weight of some big emotions on your shoulders. It's also a powerful way of acknowledging you're human and a reminder that it's perfectly OK to feel a certain way.

For example, saying "I am furious" has quite a different emphasis from "I feel furious". The former defines you as a permanently furious person whereas the latter helps you to acknowledge that you are more than your feelings. While feelings come and go, our essence remains the same.

Naming feelings in a non-judgemental way also helps to affirm self-worth and gives us the opportunity to regain power over how we feel, rather than letting the feeling run riot.

Next time you're feeling a big emotion, take a moment to name it out loud, in your head, or by writing it down on the following page.

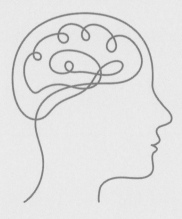

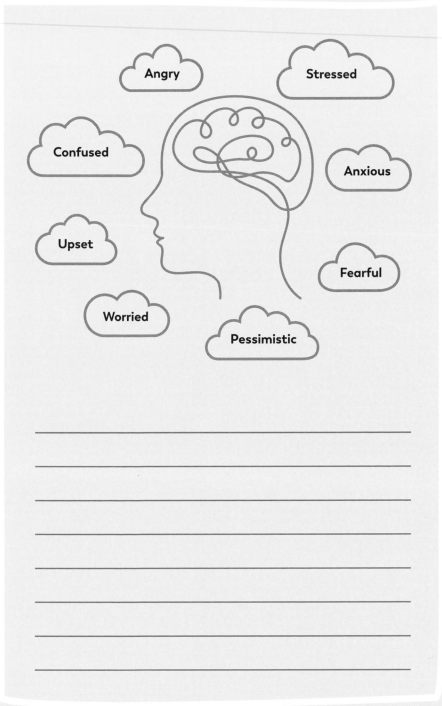

_____

_____

_____

_____

_____

_____

_____

_____

LET YOUR LOWEST
POINTS BE THE
MOTIVATION TO
MOVE ON AND MAKE
POSITIVE CHANGES

Clearing out the brain clutter

When our brains are full up with thoughts and emotions that are all jostling for attention, it can be difficult to get a bit of mental peace and quiet. It's a bit like having a cupboard that needs decluttering because every time you open the door, everything falls out. It's tempting to tell your brain to "Shut up!" at moments like this, but often that just doesn't cut it. What you need is to get comfortable with being in a "no thought" state. One of the best ways to do this is by practising meditation.

Medical research shows that long-term meditation practice helps to boost the volume and density of grey matter in your brain, improving your ability to self-regulate your emotions, as well as enhancing overall cognitive function. It also calms you down by lowering your heart rate and blood pressure. You can meditate anywhere that feels comfortable and where you won't be disturbed. The idea is to be still, physically and mentally, so a quiet spot with a chair or cushions is a good place to start.

1. Set a timer for 3 minutes or choose a relaxing song of about the same length.

2. Close your eyes. Pay attention to your breathing. Keep it slow and measured if you can.

3. Imagine your mind is a clear, blue sky. Think of your thoughts as passing clouds simply floating by, leaving the sky blue again.

4. Concentrate on your breathing and the feeling of your mind emptying. Enjoy the sensation of lightness that comes with a clearer mind.

5. When the timer runs out or the song ends, slowly open your eyes.

FIND THE CALM IN THE CHAOS

Something as simple as taking some slow deep breaths can often be enough to calm a chaotic mind. And the brilliant thing is, you don't need to be a yoga or meditation expert or need any special kit to practise deep breathing. You already have the equipment (your lungs) on standby! So, grab 10 minutes to yourself and enjoy using the power of your breath to calm yourself.

1. **Place your palms on your ribcage, paying attention to each breath you take.**

2. **Breathe in deeply through your nose then exhale through your mouth.**

3. **Feel the rise and expansion of your chest as you draw air in, and the fall as you let air out.**

4. **Concentrate on the rise and fall of your breath for 10 minutes – set a timer if you need to.**

Taking deep breaths is also great for muscle relaxation and tension relief.

You + Brain = Friends forever

Being comfortable with ourselves and who we are means making friends with our brain. We spend a lot of time in our heads and with ourselves (our whole lives in fact…), so you don't need to look any further than yourself to find true inner peace and happiness.

Making sure you get enough time alone gives you the chance to get to know yourself and what's going on inside your head without worrying about pleasing anyone else. You might think this sounds a bit lonely, particularly if you're used to being surrounded by friends, family and colleagues, but you'd be surprised how energizing it can be.

Here are some of the benefits:

◆ There's no pressure to be anything other than yourself, so you won't feel you have to be a certain way.

◆ You can explore your thoughts, feelings, values, desires, ambitions, likes, dislikes, views and beliefs away from any outside influence, which means you can get to know your true, authentic self.

◆ It can give you a chance to work through problems or challenges in your head without any outside distractions.

◆ It'll give you the space to cultivate new goals, and plan and explore new opportunities for your life.

◆ It'll help you recharge mentally, so you can re-join a hectic society with a clear head and mental strength.

◆ You'll get to spend time with someone amazing: YOU!

HOPEFUL JOURNALLING

Stress and anxiety can put a downer on even the most optimistic outlook. If you know you've got a tricky day ahead or you're feeling a little strained, try some hopeful journalling. Begin each day by visualizing the best possible outcome for yourself and write it down in this book. This will help you redirect your thoughts away from what's bothering you and towards a positive solution instead.

Think about how you'd like the day to go, what feelings you'd like to experience, what you'd like to achieve, and if you can, what you think you need to do to get positive results.

Be hopeful but realistic. Consider it as a wish list for your day. For starters, try finishing the prompts below and then use the blank space to develop those ideas further.

Today I will...

_____

_____

I'm going to feel...

_____

_____

I will achieve...

_____

_____

To do this, I will need to...

_____

_____

I will look after myself by...

_____

_____

_____

_____

_____

_____

_____

_____

_____

_____

_____

Mastering mindfulness

You might think that mindfulness is just a trend, but its benefits have been advocated by scientists for decades. But if our *mind is full*, how can *mindfulness* help? Sounds counterintuitive, right?

Our minds are amazing – that we already know. But while they are rather good at problem solving, what they're not good at is just being still and accepting what *is*.

Instead, they prefer to wander around aimlessly thinking about the past, future, what's for dinner, what the cat is doing on the fence, why your neighbour is having a party (and where was your invite?) and when you'll have time to finish that project you've been putting off all week. And that's good, because that's its job, but that sometimes means that if your mind is left to its own devices, it'll seek out new things to think about.

What mindfulness does is open the door to a mini break for your brain. It involves focusing on the present moment and using your senses to ground yourself in your body in the here and now. It can be practised as part of a meditation session or during everyday activities, like cooking, showering or walking.

If you live a busy life, mindfulness can take a bit of practice to get the hang of as you'll need to park all those distractions. But if it feels strange to begin with, don't let that put you off trying again.

Try this to start:

1. Find your nearest window. It doesn't need to be picture perfect, even a view of a concrete wall or car park will work!

2. Find a comfortable position, sitting or standing. Give your absolute full attention to what you can see outside of the window. What you can see happening outside but within the window frame is your whole universe for the next minute.

3. Study everything carefully, avoiding the use of categories or labels. Instead, aim to notice colours, textures or patterns. For instance, instead of "sky", notice the different shades of blue, white or grey, or the irregular shapes of the clouds.

4. Don't forget movement. How is the breeze blowing the grass? Or the leaves down the street?

5. Open the window. What sounds are being carried over to you? Can you smell the air?

6. Try to look at the world outside your window as though you were seeing it for the first time.

7. If you feel yourself getting distracted by other thoughts, gently steer your attention by noticing a colour or shape to bring your mind back to the present moment.

MIND FULL TO MINDFUL

How was that? Use the space below to jot down how the mindfulness exercise made you feel.

Take your time. There are prompts in the box if you need them.

> **My mind feels...**
>
> **My mind got distracted because...**
>
> **My body feels...**
>
> **I became aware of...**
>
> **I saw...**
>
> **I heard...**
>
> **I smelled...**
>
> **My focus was on...**

_____

_____

_____

_____

_____

_____

Mindful colouring

Things you need:

- Blank paper
- Colouring pencils or pens

Colour the mandala on this page. Use the moment as a mindfulness exercise, focusing on the movement of your hand across the page, the shades of the colours you choose and the texture of the paper. If you want, you could even try drawing your own on a spare piece of paper.

Anxious brain

Anxiety is our body's way of telling us that we're facing a threat. It's a completely healthy response that originates in our brain, but it affects our body too and can lead to disordered thoughts, intense emotions, faster breathing and a racing heartbeat.

The problem is that while our brains are an amazing piece of genetic engineering, they are also stuck in pre-historic times and think we're about to be mauled by a bear. When we sense danger and our brain tells our body to mobilize for action, it sends out signals in preparation to face the threat.

While it's unlikely we'll have to fight a bear any time soon, our brains are still hard-wired to help us out of sticky situations, which means that sometimes they'll spring into action if we're facing a difficult but non-life-threatening scenario – like a test or a job interview.

Most of us will experience anxiety at some point in our lives, whether it's a fleeting experience related to day-to-day stresses, for example, or whether it's a chronic condition that you learn to manage throughout your life.

We can't remove anxiety completely, but we can gather tools to cope with it, and in some situations it *can* be helpful. Anxiety often motivates us and pushes us on to achieving fantastic things – but we don't want it bothering us all the time! There are lots of simple things you can try to help you cope with anxiety, including a visualization activity on page 51 that will help you find a place of calm.

THANK YOU ANXIETY, NEXT!

When anxious thoughts are circling around our heads like a washing machine on a spin cycle, it doesn't take long for things to escalate. Often one worry leads to another, and another, and another, before circling back to the original worry, and the cycle starts all over again. Psychologists call this a "thought spiral" rather than a washing machine, and it looks like this:

I'm going to fail.

Oh no, I'm having anxious thoughts.

Get out of my mind, anxious thoughts. You're compromising my performance.

Oh no, the anxious thoughts won't go away. I'm going to do even worse.

The anxious thoughts are now even bigger. I'm now worried about doing badly.

Consider what's bothering you right now. Can your worries be solved with a practical solution?

If you already know the thought is unhelpful, you can try to simply let it go. Say in your head or out loud, "Thank you anxiety, I acknowledge that. But it's not relevant or helpful right now." Then cast the thought aside!

JOURNALLING FOR ANXIETY: PART ONE

Writing down your anxious thoughts is a brilliant way to offload your worries and replace the negative thoughts with calmer ones.

Make it an end-of-the-day habit just before you go to bed, and it'll help you to clear your mind before you go to sleep. Try this bedtime journalling exercise this evening and then try some hopeful journalling (see pages 40 and 41), freestyle journalling (see page 49) or reflective journalling (see page 63) when you're next feeling anxious.

Something that's troubling me...

_____

_____

_____

_____

What can I do to help myself with this feeling right now?

_____

_____

_____

_____

JOURNALLING FOR ANXIETY: PART TWO

Now see if you can freestyle it a little. Using the space below, aim to write about your thoughts for 5–10 minutes. You could use one of the prompts if you're struggling.

List some of the challenges you've overcome.

Write down a fear or worry and then rationalize it.

Write down something you forgive yourself for.

Write three things you'd achieve if fear wasn't a factor.

Write down one thing you look forward to every day and why.

_____

_____

_____

_____

_____

Can you think of practical steps you could take to alleviate your worries?

Or can you change your perspective from a negative to a positive?

Fact or fiction?

Anxiety can also be a bit of a truth-twister. It feeds off our negative thoughts and convinces us these are facts rather than just opinions.

True fact: I've had to work late this week and I haven't had an opportunity to spend time with my partner or catch up with friends.

Anxious "fact": I'm a total failure. I don't even deserve my partner or to have friends because I'm so unreliable.

See how sneaky that is? Anxiety takes the truth and twists it, making it a judgement of yourself. It's challenging, but we need to try to find the lesson in the anxiety and recognize that it's just an opinion, like this:

Opinion: I feel guilty that I haven't been around to spend time with my partner or friends, but I know they understand. I'll plan something nice for my partner and I this weekend, and I'll get a date in the diary for lunch with my friends. I'll learn to say "no" to working late so often.

Think of a fact that gives you anxiety and write it here.

Now think of how you can reframe this into an opinion.

IMAGINATION STATIONS

Our brains are so amazing that they can conjure images out of nothing. Making sense of how our imagination works can be the key to finding a little inner peace.

Neuroscientist Dr Andrey Vyshedskiy says that using our imagination is a complex mental action that requires precise coordination. We're able to create new images, as the brain takes familiar pieces and puts them back together in new ways, similar to how a jigsaw is assembled. This prompts the brain to start juggling a series of electrical signals to get all the images to their destination at the exact same time and create a new image in your mind.

Thousands of neurons fire in our brains when we look at an object, encoding its characteristics. For example, a pineapple is prickly, with green spiky leaves, and its fruit is yellow. All this firing strengthens the connections between neurons, and they come together in what's known as a neuronal ensemble. And then when we imagine a pineapple later, the whole ensemble lights up, forming a complete mental picture.

With all this power inside our brains, it makes sense that we should try to harness it and use it to our advantage. We can do this through visualization.

Think of a favourite spot, real or imagined, that makes you feel calm and happy: perhaps a beach at sunset, a cosy chair by a crackling fireplace, or the sunlight streaming through the forest trees. Shut your eyes and focus on details. Can you hear the waves lapping on the sand? Or smell the pine needles? Take it all in and feel the calming influence of the image quieten your mind and relax your body.

Digital detox

It's difficult to imagine a world without access to all the digital tools that we're so used to. We've all experienced that moment of horror when you realize you've left your phone somewhere you're not (or worse, lost it) and it feels a little bit like your world has just imploded. But while we've become extremely attached to the gadgets that are designed to improve our productivity, save us time and make our lives easier, often they do the exact opposite.

When did you last switch off your phone? Have you got half an eye on social media right now? Our digital tools provide a lot of distraction and make it easy for us to waste time. Spending an entire day without your phone, computer or tablet might seem quite challenging, so start by completing a 1-hour digital detox. You can always work up to longer if you find it helps. Instead, think of things you love doing that don't involve a screen!

My brain has got my back

Self-care if you're staying in

Anything you do for yourself that busts the burnout and boosts your positivity is self-care. It could be as straightforward as putting your feet up and listening to an audio book or some music. Or sitting in the garden, drinking tea and doing some mindful colouring. If it gives you confidence, raises your self-esteem and helps you access some inner peace, then you're doing it right.

Check out these ideas for things you can do at home to start cultivating all those good feels:

◆ Watch your favourite film under a blanket.

◆ Start a compliments file. Write down things people have said or say about you that make you feel warm and fuzzy inside. Read it next time you need a boost.

◆ Cook a healthy recipe and serve it up as a surprise for yourself and a loved one.

◆ Be still. Sit somewhere relaxing and be quiet for a few minutes. Just listen.

◆ Have a long bath or shower with some essential oils, sit around in your bathrobe or some joggers, and read magazines like an at-home spa day.

◆ Unplug everything for an hour and enjoy a mini digital detox.

◆ Have a dance! Put on your favourite upbeat playlist and dance like nobody's watching!

◆ Spend an hour alone doing something that feeds your mind, such as reading.

Self-care if you're heading out

Changing your scenery and heading out to do some self-care can be just as beneficial as relaxing at home. Activities such as planning an outing with friends can help you feel connected and change your mood for the better. If your self-care involves meeting up with others, make sure you surround yourself with friends who you know create a light atmosphere – it'll help to lift your mood.

Check out these ideas for things you can do when you're out to boost your mood and improve your confidence:

- Breathe some fresh air. Taking a gulp of fresh air is great for your lungs, energy levels and overall well-being.

- Go cloud-watching. Lie on your back, relax and watch the sky.

- Get some exercise. If high intensity is your thing, then running up hills is a good place to start (and you'll get a magnificent view), but even a gentle stroll through the nearest park counts.

- Walk through the woods. Being in and around nature helps us think more clearly and feel more relaxed.

- Visit a museum or art gallery. Soak up some culture, even if you don't understand what you're looking at!

- Take a different route to work, college or the shops. Mixing up your usual routine, even in a small way, helps to create new neural pathways in your brain which keeps it healthy.

- Go on a scavenger hunt. Find five beautiful things in the outside environment and take a picture of them.

MY SELF-CARE CHECKLIST

Don't forget the basics! Often it's the little things, like making sure we get enough sleep and eating properly, that contribute the most to our overall sense of well-being. Make sure you're ticking all the right boxes with this handy checklist!

Remember, these are just suggestions. You can add your own self-care needs in the blank boxes.

Self-Care Checklist

Tasks	Mon	Tue	Wed	Thur	Fri	Sat	Sun
Meditate	○	○	○	○	○	○	○
Daily gratitude practice	○	○	○	○	○	○	○
Read one chapter of a book	○	○	○	○	○	○	○
Do something creative	○	○	○	○	○	○	○
	○	○	○	○	○	○	○
	○	○	○	○	○	○	○
	○	○	○	○	○	○	○
	○	○	○	○	○	○	○

MY SELF-CARE TOOLKIT

Self-care isn't one size fits all, and your needs will be different from the next person's. Your needs will also differ day by day, depending on how you're feeling, what you've got planned, what external demands come your way and whether you're in the right frame of mind.

Use the space below to write about the things you can do daily or weekly to practise self-care. Don't forget to include the self-care you can show yourself when you're close to burnout.

Every day I can...
e.g. take a hot bath.

_____

Every week I can...
e.g. go for a nature walk.

_____

When I need a boost of confidence, I can...
e.g. look in my compliments file.

_____

When I want to show myself extra care, I will...
e.g. watch a movie under a blanket.

_____

Feeling burnt out?
Take a break

It's natural to feel a little stressed from time to time. After all, being an adult comes with a set of responsibilities, some of which are fun, some of which are not.

Work or college pressures, looking after family, financial worries, maintaining friendships and taking care of ourselves all need to be juggled just to keep things on a level. So, when something unexpected happens and we get tipped off balance it can be difficult to control our emotions. Anxiety and stress take hold and before we know it, we're heading towards an epic burnout that knocks us off our feet. We feel exhausted and overwhelmed, we become negative about everything and we start to doubt ourselves.

The way to deal with this is to learn when you need to take a break. It sounds easier said than done, but how many of us listen to what our minds and bodies are trying to tell us and act on it?

Don't wait until you feel like you're at breaking point. Recognize that self-care for your mind is a vital part of your overall well-being. Staying mentally strong, and recharging our mental batteries when we can, will help us cope with all of life's demands.

Self-care encompasses a lot of things – going for a quiet walk, doing a little gardening, spending time on a hobby – but what it isn't is self-indulgent. Take the time you need. You deserve it.

Readers of this book – know your worth!

Humans seem to be programmed to downplay their success and minimize their achievements. Most of the time this is because we fail to recognize our own abilities and efforts. We say things like "Anyone could have done it", or "I just got lucky", but by doing this we're doing ourselves and our amazing brains a disservice. This kind of mindset undermines your own hard work and success.

Start giving yourself some credit where it's due. Even reading this book up to this point means you're putting effort into improving your overall well-being. Go you! Whatever your goal is, recognize your achievements and celebrate your wins. You are amazing!

PEP-TALK YOURSELF POSITIVE

A pep talk is a bit like having a life coach living in your brain, who can motivate and inspire you in demanding situations. You can also give yourself a pep talk to remind yourself of all the things you've achieved (see page 59) and why you're capable of achieving more. You could say it either aloud or in your head – the only rule is that it's positive. And it needs to be positive and loud enough to drown out any negativity that's floating around in there.

A pep talk can be motivational or instructional, or even both! The goal is to encourage a positive outcome and boost your confidence.

One of the benefits of pep-talking yourself positive is that you don't need to rely on anyone else to deliver it – it's just there in your head whenever you need it. It'll also help you to have faith in yourself because being your own cheerleader is great for building up self-belief and a renewed sense of self-worth.

Your pep talk might sound like:

> *This is your moment to shine – you can do this. It might be tough, but you're strong and you'll see it through. Let's go!*

WRITE YOUR OWN
PEP TALK

Try writing your own pep talk in the space below.

_____

_____

_____

_____

_____

_____

_____

_____

_____

_____

_____

_____

_____

Self-reflection

Everyone has ups and downs. Some days we feel like we've achieved things – we've ticked everything off on our to-do list and life feels great – but other times we get to the end of the day and feel like we've accomplished absolutely nothing!

Spending time reflecting on our daily highs and lows can be beneficial to our mental well-being. It helps us to recognize our achievements whether they're big ("I passed my driving test") or small ("I managed to get the kids to school on time"), which is useful if you're a chronic under-estimator of your own abilities. Spend 15 minutes before bedtime asking yourself, "What have I achieved today?", and reflect on any good things that happened. Little things count just as much as big things!

REFLECTIVE JOURNALLING

Use the space below to reflect on today's highs and lows.

_____

_____

_____

_____

_____

_____

_____

_____

_____

_____

_____

_____

_____

_____

_____

Feeling like a fraud

There's an imposter lurking in many of us. Despite being capable, fully-functioning, accomplished adults, we regularly convince ourselves that we're incompetent, unintelligent, and just generally very average. We fear that at any given moment we're about to be uncovered as the massive fraudster that we are.

In fact, research suggests that at least 70 per cent of adults may experience imposter syndrome at least once in their lifetime. This research tends to focus on high-achieving individuals, but we are all plagued by doubts such as:

> Am I good enough?
>
> Do I deserve this?
>
> Why would anyone listen to me?
>
> Isn't everyone better at this than me?
>
> Doesn't everyone know more than I do?

Quite simply, we think we are fake. And bizarrely, it often gets worse when we're doing something well. The problem is, we convince ourselves that success is an all-or-nothing endeavour and then we berate ourselves when we fail to live up to our own unrealistic expectations.

To fix this, we need to let go of self-criticism and learn a little self-acceptance and self-compassion instead.

Start to retrain your focus towards a growth mindset – a mindset that actively seeks out opportunities for learning and growth. Start to see yourself as a work-in-progress rather than the finished article. Give yourself permission to be kinder to yourself – this will help you to establish more realistic expectations.

Try rephrasing your doubts so that they reflect a growth mindset, like this:

Do I need to upskill so I can achieve my goals?

What can I learn from this?

Can I do this differently next time so I can achieve a better outcome?

Can I challenge myself to go one step further?

Is there another way of looking at this challenge?

What can I learn from the people I admire?

Practise rephrasing your doubts here:

DITCH THE IMPOSTER WITH A GROWTH MINDSET

Imposter syndrome is often linked to having a fixed mindset. It causes us to believe the negative chatter our imposter is telling us which leads to a lack of resilience when we're facing a challenge or need to accept criticism.

The good news is, we can move to a growth mindset by reframing the negative thoughts from our fixed mindset with positive thoughts that will grow your self-belief. Look at the examples below and then try filling in the rest of the columns with your own ideas.

Fixed mindset thinking	Growth mindset thinking
Avoiding challenges	Embracing challenges
Giving up easily	Persisting despite obstacles
Ignoring negative feedback	Learning from criticism

Keeping track of your wins

Why do we always seem to remember what went wrong, rather than what went right? When we're grappling with imposter syndrome, we find it difficult to recognize (and remember) the role we have played in our own or others' successes.

That's why it is so important to keep track of your wins and your personal successes. Whether you've managed to work your way through some particularly difficult phone calls while caring for a grumpy baby, or you've had some brilliant feedback on a project, or you've completed some community volunteering you're proud of, or you've negotiated a seven-figure takeover deal with a global conglomerate, or some variation of all of the above (go you!), record it here for posterity. This way you can remind yourself of your amazingness whenever you need to.

What was the situation?

What was my involvement?

What challenges did I face?

What was achieved?

How did I feel afterwards?

STOP THE SELF-SABOTAGE

Self-sabotage is imposter syndrome gone rogue. When we self-sabotage, not only do we have difficulty with the idea of achieving, but we subconsciously look for ways to undermine our own progress and prevent ourselves from accomplishing our goals.

When we're caught up in this destructive mindset, our harmful behaviour can negatively impact nearly every part of our lives, including our relationships with family and friends as well as our work. In times of stress or trauma, self-sabotage can be a coping mechanism and avoidance strategy, but it often makes problems worse and limits our ability to progress towards our goals.

If you're already dealing with low self-esteem, self-sabotaging behaviour reinforces all those negative beliefs. Then, when you're close to succeeding in your goal, it makes you uncomfortable. So, you aim to fail instead, because that's what you've been telling yourself you deserve. The whole thing becomes a self-fulfilling prophecy.

Self-sabotage often falls into three categories:

- ◆ **Procrastination: Putting off working towards a good outcome because you fear that you'll disappoint others, fail or even succeed.**

- ◆ **Perfectionism: Holding unrealistic expectations hampers success as nothing will ever be "good enough", leading to a sense of disappointment.**

- ◆ **Self-Medication: Turning towards an external coping mechanism such as drugs, alcohol or self-injury to deal with uncomfortable feelings.**

So, how can we stop making our own lives more difficult?

- ◆ Stop procrastinating. Break tasks down into smaller steps so your goal isn't so overwhelming and use your pep talk whenever you need motivation.

- ◆ Stop aiming for perfection. Aim to do what is *your* best, not perfection. Don't forget, you can make improvements as you go!

- ◆ Make your goals realistic and achievable. Having a giant goal ("I want to do five marathons this month") can feel a bit overwhelming. You can dream big, but make sure your goal is realistic and your timescales are appropriate.

- ◆ Spend time examining the root causes of your behaviour. Is there a pattern of it throughout your life? If so, you may want to tackle any historical trauma or stress before trying to move forward – in which case you may want to consider professional help.

Learning how to deal with self-sabotage is the last stop on your journey towards loving your amazing mind.

Remember, you don't need to be frightened of failure anymore, because your brain will be looking out for you and cheering you on every step of the way. You've got this!

PART TWO:

Love your body

Many of us have a complicated relationship with our bodies. We tend to focus on how we look rather than all the amazing things our bodies are capable of (keeping us alive, for one!). Perhaps you're OK-ish with some bits of your body, can tolerate all the others but absolutely detest one specific part. Or maybe you're a little more accepting, and while you're not crazy about your "wobbly" bits, you'll always respect your body for carrying children, battling its way through an illness, or just simply getting you from A to B. Perhaps you unashamedly love your body – and if that's the case, feel free to pass some of that confidence around! But irrespective of how you feel, we should all agree on one thing: our bodies are amazing. Read on to find out why.

Body *bleurgh*

If you feel a bit *bleurgh* when you think about your body, you might be suffering from low body confidence.

Sometimes our negative self-talk becomes so embedded in our psyche that we just accept whatever it's telling us. But this kind of pessimistic body backchat can start to impact our daily lives. Before we know it, we've convinced ourselves we can't partake in a particular fashion trend, or participate in sports, or have our photograph taken by a loved one – all because we've fallen out of love with our body.

If you want to assess your attitude towards your body, try this little exercise. Use the space below to write ten words that describe your body.

1. _____
2. _____
3. _____
4. _____
5. _____

6. _____
7. _____
8. _____
9. _____
10. _____

Now look at them – this will help you to explore how you feel about your body.

If you've written mostly negative words and you think you struggle with low body confidence, let's try to fix that.

BODY *BLEURGH* TO BODY BEAUTIFUL

Loving your body and appreciating it for all the impressive things it does is just as important as loving your brain. The two work together in harmony to make sure that you feel like the best version of yourself every day.

Having a positive view of our bodies brings positivity to other areas of our lives – our relationships, how we perform at work or college – and gives us the confidence to achieve our goals.

Being comfortable in your body, no matter your size or shape, can free up mental energy that you can invest elsewhere – forging new relationships or nurturing existing ones, accomplishing your dreams, learning new skills and gaining knowledge, and, best of all, fostering that sense of inner peace that helps to reinforce the belief that we are amazing. Or as body image coach Jessie Barnes puts it, "It's the understanding that your appearance is simply not the most important feature of who you are as a person and that there is no such thing as a 'perfect' body."

You'll have highs and lows on your body-beautiful journey but remember that you've already done the hardest part – you've acknowledged that you want to feel better about yourself. We only get one body, so it's time to start loving it!

"Perfect body" myth busting

Time for an important announcement. Drumroll, please...

THERE IS NO SUCH THING AS A PERFECT BODY!

You have your body and other people have theirs. That's the simple truth of the matter.

Unfortunately, social media, the internet, TV, film, magazines, advertising and all the other image-laden media we're surrounded by every day have other ideas. Apparently, they think they do know what a perfect body looks like – and they seem to enjoy telling us it isn't ours.

If your body confidence is already on the low side and you don't value your own opinions or have the confidence to question other people's, then this can be a bit of a problem. It leaves you vulnerable to falling into the trap of believing everything you consume. Before you know it, that little critical voice that lives inside your mind is wearing you down to the point where you've convinced yourself that to be socially acceptable, you must strive to achieve this mythical "perfect body".

In these moments, remember this: your body is worthy of your care and compassion as it is. Recognize your body's value – and celebrate its uniqueness. Your body is amazing!

Low mood, low body confidence

If you're struggling with low mood, you might also find you struggle with low body confidence. It's normal to feel low or down from time to time and it's not always an indicator that something is wrong in your life. Sometimes low mood just sneaks up on us and we begin to feel a little tired and deflated. Our confidence wanes, we get easily frustrated or even angry and anxiety may take hold. As a result, your opinion of yourself and how you look can take a bit of a battering.

At times like these, the best thing to do is to try to be super kind to yourself. One of the ways we can do this is by developing a friendly and patient inner voice that can support us through these low periods. Explore how your inner voice can become your best friend on pages 76 and 77.

BECOMING YOUR OWN BEST FRIEND

Think back to a time when you felt as though your mood had hit rock bottom.

How did that make you feel? Did it crush your self-confidence? Perhaps it affected your self-worth, and your inner voice was being a bit of a bully.

Write down your thoughts and feelings about that time here.

_____

_____

_____

_____

_____

_____

_____

_____

_____

BULLY TO BEST FRIEND

If your inner voice is contributing to your low mood and how you feel about yourself, it's time to teach it how to show a little more compassion!

What would you say to that past version of yourself to be more supportive?

Imagine you are speaking to a friend or loved one. You might say "You've got amazing resilience, I wish I was as brave as you". Or you could even think about what you would say to a friend if they needed a body-confidence boost: "You're worth so much more than your appearance."

Try writing what you would say to yourself to be more caring.

_____

_____

_____

_____

_____

_____

_____

_____

_____

_____

_____

Body-confident affirmations

As we explored on page 30, affirmations are short, positive statements that help to inspire and lift us up when we need a boost of positivity. They're also a helpful tool for resetting how we feel and think about ourselves and our bodies. And, if we say them to ourselves enough, we start to believe them.

Use the affirmations below to try it yourself. Try to really feel and hear the message they are telling you for maximum effect.

My body is amazing. It does amazing things

I commit to listening to my body's needs

My value as a person does not change with my weight

I am not defined by my appearance

I am tuned in to what my body needs

A "perfect" body is one that's keeping me alive

I am more than the number on the scales

I define my own beauty

My body deserves love and respect

I am strong and capable

My body-love affirmations

Now it's your turn. Only you know what you want to achieve in terms of body positivity, so writing some of your own body-love affirmations will give you the opportunity to create statements that really resonate with you. Use the space below to jot some down.

And you are?

Things you need:

- Paper
- Pen
- Colouring pencils (optional)
- Stickers (optional)

The essence of who you are as a person has absolutely nothing to do with your body or what it looks like. Now we've cleared that up, it's time you started seeing yourself as the amazing person you are.

Grab a pen and some paper and write a list of all the things you are. Perhaps you're a loyal friend, a caring mother, a maths whizz or the life and soul of the party...

Then, try to write ten things you love about yourself. There might be some crossover between things you are, such as spontaneous, and things you love about yourself, such as your spontaneity. Perhaps you could link these on the page.

If you're feeling creative, you could add some drawings and stickers around your words.

You could display your list somewhere you will see it every day. The more you read it, the more it'll sink in!

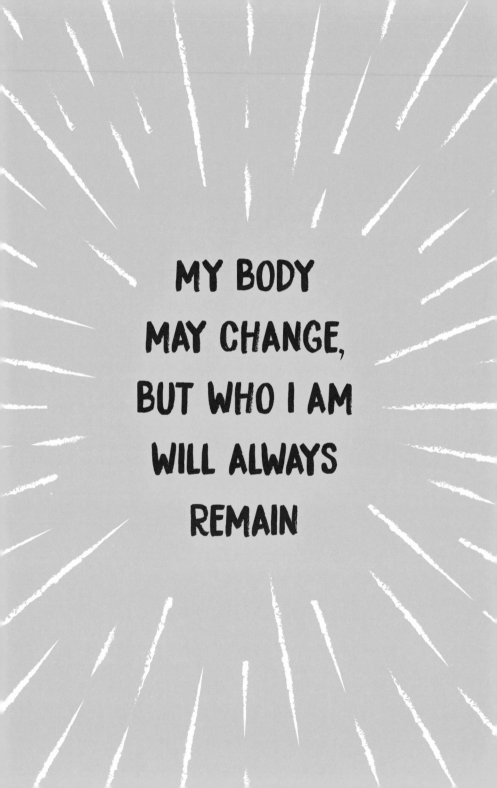

Cultivate your self-love

Putting aside the time to work on your relationship with yourself will boost your mood as well as feelings of self-connection. Try to work some of these self-love actions into your life – and remember, it's always OK to make time for yourself and prioritize cultivating your self-love.

◆ **Enjoy some solitude. You could just sit quietly with your thoughts or go for a walk in your favourite space. Connect with yourself and know that you deserve this time for yourself.**

◆ **Listen to calming music. Studies show the benefits of music include lower blood pressure, reduction of stress, a feeling of relaxation and a boost in mood and brain function.**

◆ **Start a self-love journal and aim to fill it in every day. Try to list three things you were grateful for today and something you did today that made you proud.**

◆ **Try some brain-boosting techniques such as meditation (see page 37) and mindfulness (see pages 42 and 43). Being aware of our body, heartbeat and breathing can help reduce stress, clear our mind of clutter and refocus our thoughts.**

◆ **Find joy in movement. Choose something that you enjoy – the aim is to feel better rather than change how you look. Yoga, dancing, walking and even chair-based exercises can all help boost your mood. Knowing your body's strengths and what makes it feel good is all part of growing a relationship with yourself. And moving is great for overall health too!**

I ♡ me

Cultivating love for ourselves goes hand in hand with self-care. Taking time out to do something that makes us feel good about ourselves is the ultimate expression of self-love. But to genuinely love yourself, you need to get under your own skin a little and understand yourself in a way that no one else does. Connecting with yourself on a more meaningful level helps you to accept who *you* are, meaning you have a much better chance of being kind to yourself when you're finding life tough.

Learning to love, respect and trust yourself is like reaching the pinnacle of positivity. You'll find a sense of inner peace and calm that perhaps you've never had before. In turn, this will lead to a renewed sense of resilience when you come up against your next challenge.

I AM WHO I AM

From self-love grows self-awareness. When we can see clearly who we are – our values, desires, beliefs, thoughts, and feelings – through introspection, we increase our self-awareness. From self-awareness comes a sense of confidence and belief in ourselves that makes us feel comfortable with who we are. It's also important to consider how other people see us. This increases our external self-awareness and our understanding of other people's perceptions.

Find a quiet spot and try answering these questions. You can either write your answers in the space provided or separately in a notepad or journal of your own. There are no right or wrong answers. Just aim for honesty!

How do you think your closest friend or a member of your family would describe you in three sentences?

_____

_____

_____

If a loved one were writing your biography, what kinds of things would they mention?

_____

_____

_____

Now, put others' perspectives aside for a moment and answer these questions.

If you were writing to your past self, what would you say about who you are now?

_____

_____

_____

Imagine you're writing to your future self. How would you describe what makes you, you?

_____

_____

_____

Now you have a set of answers, have a think about the following:

◆ Does anything stand out from your answers? Has anything surprised you?

◆ How has the activity made you feel?

◆ Have you learned anything about yourself?

◆ Are there any steps you can take to keep growing your self-awareness?

Jot down your responses below.

_____

_____

_____

TRUST IN YOUR BODY

It's a sad fact that sometimes the basic needs of our body fall to the bottom of the priority list. We get busy and we forget to eat, or we don't notice that we haven't had something to drink all afternoon. Or maybe we're so busy with work that we can't take a break when we need it. Sometimes we barely have time to go to the toilet when we need to!

When we ignore what our body is telling us and push those thoughts away, we're not showing ourselves compassion. And part of this is down to trust. When we trust our body, we understand what feels normal for us and we listen and act on our body's cues, such as hunger, thirst, fatigue and, yes, even going to the toilet promptly.

Trust is an essential component of every relationship and it's no different for the relationship you have with your body. If we trust in our body, it will reward us with a renewed sense of mental and physical well-being.

To nurture trust in your body, try the following activities:

◆ Don't ignore your body signals. Make a conscious effort to notice feelings of hunger, tiredness, feeling unwell, and so on. Ask yourself what your body needs to help the feeling go away.

◆ Be mindful of your inner critic contradicting you or telling you that you can't. For example, "You have to finish the washing up before you can have lunch" or "You can't eat that until you've exercised first." Don't let your inner voice drown out your body cues.

◆ Respect your body by doing what it is asking of you. You owe it to your body, and it'll pay you back in dividends.

Don't belittle your body

If you're the kind of person who openly criticizes themselves in conversations, you're not doing your body confidence any favours! Throwaway comments we make to other people might seem innocuous, but as humans we tend to internalize what we verbalize. This means that if we say these negative things often enough, they become part of our belief system.

It's so easy to slip into talking about our bodies when we're with friends, and chatting about health concerns in a safe space with people we love can often be extremely beneficial. But if you're finding that these chats are simply becoming an opportunity for you all to complain about things you don't like about yourselves, it might be time to change the record. After all, you've got more to offer than your appearance!

The next time you're in this situation, try the following:

◆ Note the conversation has shifted to making disparaging comments about your own bodies. Did anything trigger it?

◆ How do the words you're saying make you feel?

◆ Challenge those comments in your head. Are they unhelpful? Unnecessary? Are you just trying to get a laugh?

◆ Shift the conversation onto another topic. Make a promise with yourself (if you can get your friends on board, even better!) that going forward you'll talk about other things, rather than expending any energy criticizing your appearance.

Body-confidence goals

Goal setting is an important part of any well-being journey. It gives us something to aim for, which helps to motivate us to stay on track. And when we can see ourselves achieving our goal in real time, it gives us a confidence boost.

Think about some of the goals that you'd like to achieve to feel better about your body. Perhaps you lack confidence with something specific you'd like to overcome, or you might have something more generic in mind. Allow yourself to prioritize these goals and recognize that through achieving them, you'll be serving your long-term health and happiness.

My body-confidence goals

Use the space below to jot down some ideas for what you would like to achieve in the next week, month, year or more. Use the prompts if you need them.

I want to worry less about...

_____

I want to feel less self-conscious about...

_____

I want to feel more confident when I...

_____

I want to overcome my fear of...

_____

I want to be able to...

_____

Every day I want to wake up feeling...

_____

VISUALIZE YOURSELF BEING BODY CONFIDENT

We looked at visualization for inner peace on page 51, but we can use the same process to nurture body confidence too. Visualizing ourselves being confident in our own skin can be incredibly motivating because it allows us a glimpse of what body confidence feels like. It also helps to build new neural pathways in our brain, so we can re-wire a negative mindset into a positive one.

The first step to getting those neurons firing is to use a little imagination. Answer the following questions.

Imagine you've got unlimited body confidence...

What are you doing? Think about what activities you'd have the confidence to try, like going to the gym or swimming, or even being more intimate with your partner.

_____

_____

_____

What are you thinking? Are you admiring your body's strength and health? Perhaps you're thinking how much you like it.

_____

_____

_____

What are you feeling? Do you feel happy? Free? Confident?

_____

_____

_____

Now imagine you're doing one of the activities you've identified...

Close your eyes and immerse yourself in the experience. Feel the freedom that body confidence has given you. Notice what you're thinking. How does this feel different to the way you usually are?

_____

_____

_____

Imagine "current you" in that same situation. How could you channel some of "other you's" body confidence? What's their secret?

_____

_____

_____

Use this scenario whenever you need a boost of confidence or visualize it every day for maximum effect. You could try visualizing yourself doing different activities. The aim is to create a more positive attitude towards your body.

MY BODY-CONFIDENCE ROLE MODEL

Some people just exude confidence. We all "know" at least one person who seems to be totally rocking the whole body-confidence thing. Perhaps you've got a friend who wears funky, eye-catching outfits for everything. Or you admire your partner for being able to don their beach attire without so much as a second thought.

Having a body-confidence role model can be useful for nurturing your own self-love. It's not about wishing your appearance was like theirs or wanting to emulate their body. Instead, choose someone who inspires you to be authentically yourself. Who would you choose?

Mind mapping the words you associate with your role model can help. These might be adjectives, song lyrics, quotes or things they've achieved. Next time your confidence is feeling a little shaky, imagine they are with you, radiating self-belief and mentoring you to be your most confident self.

MY STRATEGY FOR SUCCESS

While all goals are different, especially when we're thinking about body confidence, they all have something in common: a strategy can be the best way to help you achieve them.

Sounds like challenging work, but guess what? You've already done most of that! By reading this far and following some of the advice, you've probably already got some ideas about the best way to reach your goal. Have a flip back through the pages in this book for inspiration and fill the boxes in below.

Date:

Goal:

Steps:

Date:

Goal:

Steps:

Date:

Goal:

Steps:

Check your body language cues

Is your body language fluent in confidence?

How confident we look and feel is projected through our body language. This means that if we feel great, we're more likely to hold our heads high, strut down the street and act confidently.

The problem is, if we don't feel confident, our body language will reflect how we're feeling inside: we hunch our shoulders, hang our heads and try to shrink into ourselves so we don't have to interact with the world. And that's fine if you're having an off day and can't cope with adulting right now, but if this is you all the time then there are some simple steps you can take to develop more confident body language. By doing so, you'll start to feel more confident inside too. Hurrah!

- Make good eye contact. This shows you're attentive and are confident enough to hold your own in a conversation.

- Stand up straight. Imagine someone is pulling you up with a golden thread. This'll lift your mood and help to build inner confidence.

- Use open hand gestures to display your palms and keep your hands out of your pockets. This'll show others you have confidence in what you're saying, and will help to build trust with people.

- Avoid crossing your arms. This can indicate feelings of insecurity or despondency.

- Relax and smile. Focus on what you're doing and saying instead of worrying about what other people think of you.

Body neutrality – what's that?

You don't have to love everything about your body. Loving your body isn't about forcing yourself to have a better relationship with the things you really dislike. There's nothing useful to be gained from faking an appreciation of your nose if you've spent the last 25 years wishing you could afford to have cosmetic surgery on it. Aim for toleration – AKA body neutrality.

Feeling indifferent about your body is fine – your worth doesn't lie in your appearance – and although body image does contribute to how we perceive ourselves, it isn't everything.

Base your self-perception on other parts of yourself instead: what a great friend you are, how your body helps you be an amazing dancer, what a fantastic imagination you have, what a formidable problem solver you are, how you never give up even when obstacles try to stop you...

It's what's inside that counts

Judging the bodies of everyone around you is just as negative as judging your own. Even if we just say it in our heads rather than out loud, it doesn't make it any better.

It's not just an unkind, negative way of thinking, but that same voice in your head that's judging everyone else is the same voice you use to judge yourself. Which means that if that voice is super nasty, you're probably going to be saying some horrible things to yourself too.

Next time you hear your inner voice being judgemental, check yourself by trying the following:

◆ Focusing on the person inside the body rather than their body itself. Are they funny? Kind? Switched on? Friendly?

◆ Not comparing their body to yours or anyone else's. No one asked for your assessment or opinion, so try not to give it (yes, that includes in your head!). Remember that we are all unique. Counteract that comparative voice with a complimentary one.

◆ Challenging the thought. Are you just projecting your perception of yourself on to them? If you're poking fun at someone's body shape, is it possible you're feeling insecure about your own? If so, take steps to work on your own confidence rather than allowing unkind thoughts about somebody else's appearance to occupy your headspace.

My mind is free from worrying about what other people think of me

DIVE INTO DIVERSITY

If we know that constant exposure to what the media considers to be the "perfect" body type (see page 74) leads to a negative impact on our own body confidence, then it makes sense that we can offset this by exposing ourselves to environments that advocate for body positivity instead.

Seek out opportunities where you can expose yourself to people of all ages, ethnicities, shapes and sizes, and from different cultures and backgrounds.

If we can normalize our experience of living with our own unique body, we become more accepting of not only the body we've been given but the diversity of other bodies around us too.

Start by raising your own body awareness of the people around you. Don't stare at other people but do note to yourself that if you look around, no one actually fits the so-called "ideal" shape.

Follow social media accounts that reflect body positivity. You'll know which ones are right for you because you'll be able to spot your own body type among the images they feature.

Lastly, if you feel confident enough, you could start your own Instagram or Pinterest account that showcases body diversity. The louder we all shout about body positivity, the better it will be for everyone.

Defining beauty

What does "beautiful" look like to you? If we consider how beauty is portrayed in the media, it's something that is entirely appearance-based and fails to recognize our internal qualities, or body diversity. When we accept this limited view, we set ourselves up for a lifetime of dissatisfaction with our own appearance.

If we construct our own definition of beauty, we can take back control and stop worrying about what society thinks "beauty" looks like, which means we'll be less likely to compare ourselves unfavourably. Think about your friends, family, and all the other amazing people in your life. What qualities do they have that makes them "beautiful" to you?

Find the people who lift you up... and then never let them go!

Surrounding yourself with good people, those that lift you up and encourage you to be the best version of yourself, is like winning the relationship lottery.

Not only will they help to safeguard your self-confidence, but they'll always be there when you need a kind word, a loving arm to lean on (or shoulder to cry on) and a boost of empowerment when life is wearing you down.

You'll be able to spot these people from a mile away because they're the ones cheering loudly for you from the sidelines as you journey through life. Most importantly, they accept you as you are, even when you've done something regrettable or you say something ridiculous. They've got your back.

The more you surround yourself with the right people for you, people who demonstrate all these qualities and more, the more confident you'll become in recognizing what you value in future relationships.

You'll also get better at spotting the bad apples and weeding them out. Part of life is accepting you'll lose friends along the way – people change and move on – but the ones that stick around are the ones who are worth hanging on to. So never let them go!

MY CHEERLEADERS

Your support network can be made up of anyone who brings positivity to your life, whether you're riding high or going through turbulent times. They might be friends, family members, neighbours or colleagues.

In the space below, write down the people who empower you to feel your best. Underneath you can use the space to write about how they do this, what support they provide and why you value having them in your life so much.

The people who empower me are...

_____

_____

They support me by...

_____

_____

They raise my confidence because...

_____

_____

I value them so much because...

_____

_____

COPING WITH NEGATIVE COMMENTS

If there's one thing we don't need in our lives, it's judgemental comments from other people. We give ourselves enough of a hard time without having someone else reinforcing that negativity.

Whether it's to your face, online or on social media, this kind of behaviour isn't just unacceptable. Part of building up body confidence is learning how to value your body, even when other people clearly don't. And this means calling that person, or people, out.

Irrespective of who has delivered the comment, your body is your business, and if they've said something that has upset you, then that's not on.

Next time you're faced with this scenario, try the following:

1. State calmly and unemotionally that you find their comments upsetting, such as, "You've mentioned several times recently that my body is an unhealthy size, and I ought to lose weight. I want to tell you how I feel about it."

2. Next, tell them how their behaviour has impacted you. Try to avoid stating that it's "made" you feel so it doesn't come across as accusatory and put them on the defensive. Instead, use "I" statements such as, "When you say comments like that, I feel upset and angry."

3. Lastly, politely ask them to change their behaviour, such as, "I'm asking that you stop making these comments now." If they don't, you might need to stop seeing them for a while or you may need to cut them from your life completely if they continue to have a negative impact.

Dealing with a toxic relationship

Many of us have at least one horror story from our past where a relationship has gone sour because someone has made us feel as though we're not good enough. Whether it's a friend, loved one or even a close family member who is damaging your self-esteem, if you surround yourself with people who constantly belittle you it's hardly surprising that you'll start to believe all the negativity yourself. If you're in a toxic relationship that's starting to have a negative impact on how you feel about yourself, keep the following in mind:

◆ **Aim for healthy communication. Talk to them honestly about how they are making you feel and (tempting though it may be) try not to be unkind in return. Let them know how their behaviour has affected your confidence.**

◆ **Work out your boundaries. Discuss what is OK and what isn't. Remember boundaries change over time, so it's important to keep discussing them openly, particularly if the relationship is damaged and you're trying to rebuild it.**

◆ **Give each other time and space. Repairing a toxic relationship won't happen overnight. Make sure you allow time for each other to change and grow.**

◆ **End the relationship. If you feel the relationship still isn't working or your feelings and boundaries have not been respected, it may be time to call time on it. This is never an easy decision but know that any short-term heartache is worth enduring if your future will look brighter as a result. Draw on support from people who make you feel good about yourself and know that better days are on the horizon.**

Under pressure

It's a sad fact of society that certain, often unrealistic, body types are idealized.

It's nothing new, after all women have been squeezing themselves into corsets and other shape-training contraptions for centuries, but the proliferation of social media means we see other people's bodies more than ever before. Couple those images with creative lighting, filters, and the ability to like, comment and follow for additional validation, it's no wonder most of us feel that we just don't measure up.

And this issue doesn't just affect one group. Everyone can feel the pressure to look a certain way due to the messages we are exposed to. Although the most significant effects of the media on body image and self-esteem have been observed in women, men are not immune to the effects of the "perfect" body.

Men are more likely to believe that a muscular body helps to reinforce their strength and masculinity. Statistics from a recent Australian study show that the percentage of men dissatisfied with their body image tripled in the last 25 years, from 15 per cent of the population to 45 per cent.

The reality is that most of what we see in the media – specifically social media – is a very carefully curated snapshot of someone's life.

Most of us don't post images of ourselves dressed in joggers and sprawled on the sofa eating pizza or sitting slouched at our desk working our way through emails and our third cup of coffee. This creates a toxic environment in which only a very small percentage of people get attention for what they look like for only a very small amount of their daily lives. We just can't help but compare ourselves, which always leaves us feeling as though we can't possibly measure up.

What we need to do is stop ruminating over the things we don't like about our bodies and start recognizing all the fantastic stuff it does instead.

Some fantastic things my body does:

Unfollow and unfriend

There are things you can do right now to start improving your body confidence.

We spend so much of our day endlessly scrolling through social media that it's the easiest place to start making a difference. And apart from feeling better about yourself, you'll be surprised just how much time you gain too!

Every time you see a post that makes you feel bad about your body or how you look, just hit the "unfollow" or "see fewer posts like this" button. If it's someone you know in real life, you could just "hide" their posts instead.

Taking straightforward steps like this to prevent us falling into the social media "comparison trap" will help us to banish body negativity and unhelpful self-talk.

It'll also build up your confidence as you're taking back control of what you want to see, rather than the unfathomable social media algorithms deciding for you. You are not obliged to follow anyone. Don't forget that.

Once you've sent all the people making you feel rubbish about yourself to the sin bin, replace them with people who do the opposite!

NOW WHAT? THINGS TO DO INSTEAD OF SCROLLING SOCIAL MEDIA

It's surprising how much time you can save from not being on social media. With this new free time, you'll have the perfect opportunity to do all the things that make you feel amazing.

Make a list below of some of the things you'll fill your time with as well as a few ideas for things you haven't ever tried but would like to.

_____

_____

_____

_____

_____

_____

_____

_____

Social media – the root of all evil?

OK – maybe that's a bit of an exaggeration. After all, social media allows us to be, well, *social*. And that's a good thing, right?

It means that at a touch of a few buttons we can see what our friends, family and loved ones are getting up to, what they're achieving, how they're feeling, where they are, what sort of a day they're having, and so on. We can check in with everyone we hold dear and look through a metaphorical window into their lives.

While social media has transformed the way we connect with the people we share our lives with, as well as acquaintances, colleagues, favourite celebrities, influencers, brands and just about the entire population of the world, it also has the potential to be a toxic environment, particularly if you're feeling vulnerable and have low confidence.

The fact that social media platforms are primarily image-led also adds to our woes. The temptation to compare how we look to other people, particularly those we may look up to, is strong. But obsessing over other people's appearances, especially if you are unhappy with your own, will inevitably lead to you feeling worse about yourself. Comparison isn't just a thief of joy, it's a total pain as well.

We *could* blame all of society's ills on social media, and it's tempting, but it's not all bad news. Used wisely (see pages 98 and 106 for some ideas), social media can be a great source of information, relaxation and entertainment. We just need to make sure we're using it in a positive, balanced way.

Seven-day social media detox

Several studies have shown that even if you just take a mini break from social media, it can reduce anxiety and boost our overall feeling of well-being. There are a few different ways you can limit your time spent on social media, including apps that help you to keep track of your usage, but a good place to start is to have a bit of a detox.

To help you do that, use the tracker below. Don't forget to put a big tick through each day you achieve your goal.

Day one Switch off all social media notifications	**Day two** Unsubscribe and unfollow people you don't know and accounts that make you feel negative about yourself
Day three No social media until 9 a.m.	**Day four** No scrolling after 8 p.m.
Day five Have 3 hours of screen-free time	**Day six** No social media until 5 p.m.
Day seven No social media all day. You're officially a social-media-free zone until tomorrow!	

DON'T PLAY THE NUMBERS GAME

It isn't just images on social media that can make us feel bad about how we look.

When we focus on numbers it can be triggering too. Whether it's the weight on the scales, the size on your clothes, how many steps you've done today, and so on – whatever information your gadgets are feeding back to you can sometimes do more harm than good.

Measuring our gym performance, our eating habits and how long we spend moving or sitting down can be helpful for making sure we're staying healthy, but if it's having a detrimental effect on our mental well-being and we're starting to obsess over our daily statistics, we need to stop looking at them!

Numbers don't define what a happy and healthy version of your body looks like. They're just numbers, and they don't account for how you're feeling or what you've been doing on any given day. Those numbers can look pretty judgemental at times, so learn to listen to your body and how it's feeling instead.

Eat when you're hungry, sleep when you're tired, and be active in ways that suit you and make you feel good about yourself. You can trust your body to take care of the rest.

Feed your brain

Eating well not only helps our body stay strong and healthy, but it nourishes our brain too. If our body and brain are happy, it helps *us* to feel happy and confident, and aids in combatting those "hangry" feelings, i.e. when we get a little irritable and lack energy. This is because if we don't eat regularly our blood sugar level drops, making us tired, moody and unable to concentrate, whereas if we keep our blood sugar levels consistent, we're more likely to maintain a positive frame of mind throughout the day (and keep everyone around us happy too!).

Food is fuel

Our body deserves our respect, so make sure you're showing it some by developing good eating habits. This, of course, is easier said than done, but even little tweaks such as cutting back on sugar in your coffee or prioritizing protein can make a substantial difference.

You don't need to do anything radical if you want to improve your diet. Instead, eat for energy, strength and overall well-being. Remember, food is fuel!

According to the World Health Organization, a healthy adult diet contains protein, fruit, vegetables, legumes (such as lentils and beans), nuts and whole grains (such as unprocessed maize, millet, oats, wheat and brown rice), as well as a little sugar, fat and carbs – and we should aim to include these in our three main meals of the day.

If you're partial to a snack or two, those that are high in vitamins and release energy slowly are best for avoiding that hangry feeling when your blood sugar drops, and irritability strikes! Probiotic yoghurt, mixed nuts with dried fruit, wholewheat crackers, bananas on toast, or toast with peanut butter are all good options if you need a body and brain boost.

Don't forget to stay hydrated too! Scientific research shows that even mild dehydration can impair our memory and mood, as well as being detrimental to our body. If you find it difficult to keep your liquid levels up, why not treat yourself to a funky water bottle and aim to refill it at least twice during the day?

FUEL TRACKER

Keep track of the food you're fuelling your body with using the table below. Ensure you're getting all the nutritional goodness you need for both body and brain health.

	What I fuelled with	How I felt after
Mon		
Tue		
Wed		
Thur		
Fri		
Sat		
Sun		

DON'T FALL INTO THE DIET TRAP

According to research published in the *British Medical Journal*, a whopping 95 per cent of diets fail. So why is dieting still such a hot topic?

The reality is, if diets really worked, the diet industry simply wouldn't exist anymore. We'd all be our "ideal" weight and would have no need for them!

Faddy diets that involve intermittent fasting, existing on food supplements or juice shakes, or only eating one type of food group and excluding all others are largely created to make profits rather than promote body confidence. Since dieting, by definition, is a temporary food plan, it won't work in the long run – and you might end up unhappier than when you started.

Focus on your overall health instead. If you want a doughnut, eat it guilt free. If you fancy some fruit instead, go for that. Listen to your body's needs and honour them. Pay attention to how you feel after eating certain foods. Prioritize those that you enjoy and that help you work towards your wellness goals.

No one is ever remembered for being really good at dieting. Be memorable because you're a fabulous friend or warm-hearted individual and make your legacy a healthy approach to looking after your body, rather than a legacy of punishment through dieting.

THERE IS NO
SUCH THING AS
"GOOD" FOOD OR "BAD"
FOOD; FOOD IS JUST
THE FUEL WE NEED
TO STAY HEALTHY

Dress to impress

If you've fallen out of love with your body, you might be trying to hide it away.

You might just chuck on the first thing you see hanging in the wardrobe that gives your body the most coverage or makes you as inconspicuous as possible – think drab, oversized jumpers and tatty sweatpants. But if your clothes are screaming dull rather than dynamic, it won't be helping to build up your body confidence.

Your body is amazing and it's beautiful, and it deserves to look and feel its best! Next time you throw open your wardrobe, aim for clothes that'll lighten up the room as well as your mood.

It's not about how you look, it's about how you *feel*, so dress in clothes that make you smile. Think about the textures you like against your skin, the patterns and prints you enjoy and the styles you want to try. You don't even need to overhaul your wardrobe – you can change up an outfit with some funky accessories or different colour combinations.

If you're concerned about body image, you might have convinced yourself that you can't wear a certain outfit until your body looks a certain way, but why wait? If you know wearing a particular outfit will make you feel amazing, start wearing it now.

There are some practical steps you can take too. Go into your wardrobe and throw out or donate everything that makes you feel bad about yourself.

Just remember, it's not about being on trend. It's about expressing yourself and what you're all about. You deserve to love the clothes, and body, you're in.

Amazing sleep = amazing you

Isn't going to sleep amazing? Sinking into a warm, cosy bed (bonus good-feels if the sheets are freshly cleaned) and drifting off to slumberland is the epitome of wonderfulness.

Not only is sleep imperative for our brain – it helps our minds to recharge, embed our memories into longer-lasting knowledge and process our thoughts – but it's critical for a happy body too. It gives our body a chance to repair and renew itself, as well as giving it that all important chance to take a break and get our energy levels back up again, ready for the next day.

And who doesn't feel like they can take on the world after a decent bit of shut-eye?

The problem is, our lives can make this quite difficult. Stress, anxiety, too much light coming in through the curtains, unruly children and pets, a restless partner, outside noises, getting too hot or feeling too cold are all things that love to interfere with a decent night's sleep.

Not only will this make it difficult for us to control our emotions during our waking hours, but bad-quality sleep can make your positivity plummet.

The rule is: the more consistent your sleep cycle, the better you will feel – meaning you'll be in the right frame of mind to be body confident. And if our bodies feel happy, it's that bit easier for us to love them!

My night-time routine

Developing a good night-time routine is the key to a good night's sleep. According to the National Sleep Foundation, adults aged 18–60 need 7–9 hours of sleep per night. Some of us need a little more, some a little less.

You can maximize your chances of getting all the sleep you need by following a few simple habits:

◆ Make sure your sleep environment is as relaxing as possible. Reduce noise and distractions and make sure your bedroom is at an optimal temperature.

◆ Establish a healthy pre-bedtime routine. Having good bedtime habits sends your body sleep signals so that it starts to wind down.

◆ Try to go to sleep at the same time every night. This will help get your body clock into a regular rhythm for sleep.

What's your night-time routine?

Jot down the things you like to do to prepare for your sleep journey.

MY SLEEP TRACKER

Record your sleep habits using the tracker below. Look for any patterns, such as did you sleep better on the days you exercised? Or did you work late and then have a disturbed night because you couldn't mentally switch off? If so, there's a good chance there are some simple lifestyle adjustments you can make to improve the quality of your sleep.

Complete in the morning							
Today's date							
Time I went to bed last night							
Time I woke up this morning							
Time it took to fall asleep							
Things I did yesterday							
How awake I feel now							

Marvellous movement

While we know we *should* take regular exercise – because it's good for us and all that – sometimes it's not an overly joyful experience. We get hot. We get sweaty. It makes us tired. We might get an injury or pull a muscle. We feel bad because everyone else seems to enjoy it, but we don't. And so on, and so forth.

If you're finding that your usual exercise regime has become more painful than pleasurable, it's probably time to switch to something you're going to enjoy.

What's the answer? Choose physical activities that you *want* to do, rather than those you think you *should*. You'll be more motivated to keep up the good habit, and it'll bring a ton of positive benefits to not just your physical health but your mental and emotional well-being too.

If you're struggling to think of some ideas, consider the following to help you choose:

> ◆ What did you enjoy as a child? Would any of these activities work for you now?
>
> ◆ What do your friends, family or loved ones do? Would you like to try any of their activities?
>
> ◆ What activity have you always wanted to try but haven't? It's never too late to learn something new!

If getting out is a struggle, there are lots of gentle home-based exercise programmes you can try online or through an app which you can follow at your own pace.

MOVEMENT TRACKER

You can keep track of your movement activities here. You could always set yourself a few weekly goals such as "spend at least half an hour every day doing active movement", or "go for a walk three times".

Day	Movement	Time spent	How it made me feel
Mon			
Tue			
Wed			
Thur			
Fri			
Sat			
Sun			

BODY GRATITUDE = BODY ACCEPTANCE

There is so much more to your body than how it looks. When was the last time you really stopped and appreciated all the hard work your body does for you daily? For example, by the end of today, do you know your lungs will have taken over 20,000 breaths?

Showing your body a bit of gratitude every now and again for all the incredible things it allows you to accomplish will help you to nurture a more balanced view of yourself. Try this for starters:

Body gratitude

I am grateful for this body.

It allows me to _____

My face radiates _____

My eyes are filled with _____

My lips help me _____

I am grateful for hands and arms that _____

With this stomach I can _____

These hips and legs allow me to _____

My feet are _____

The bigger picture

Body confidence is important, but it shouldn't be confused with self-worth. If you want to start truly loving the body you've been given, you need to see the bigger picture – which means focusing on yourself as a whole. It's great to accept (and possibly even love) your physical attributes, but you also need to remember that housed inside your amazing body are all the qualities that make you unique.

I love the person I am on the outside because...

I love the person I am on the inside because...

Ten things I love about me:

1.
2.
3.
4.
5.
6.
7.
8.
9.
10.

DEAR YOUNGER ME... YOU ARE AMAZING!

Many insecurities over our appearance stem from childhood and adolescence when we're a little vulnerable. This is largely due to the combination of hormones, working out who we are and what we're about and being susceptible to peer pressure and the opinions of others.

If you could go back and talk to your younger self, what would you say?

Let's take a trip back to the mind of younger you. How did you feel? What body worries concerned you? Was anything happening in your life at the time that might have triggered those anxious feelings?

Write anything you can think of here.

Write a letter to your younger self. Think about what you needed to hear back then. Perhaps you could have used some reassurance that you were perfect just as you were, or that you're amazing inside and out.

Use words of comfort and kindness to let your "little you" know everything's going to be OK.

Dear younger me,

_____

_____

_____

_____

_____

_____

_____

_____

_____

_____

_____

_____

_____

Saying farewell to your "ideal" body

It's going to be tough, but you need to say goodbye to something close to you. You've been through good times and bad (mostly bad) times, you've invested heavily in shared dreams and ambitions, but it's time to cut it loose – you need to let go of your "ideal" body.

If you're still striving for it, or worse, waiting for it to make you happier, more successful and more fulfilled, then you definitely need to let it go. All the time your imagined future is conditional on an "ideal" you're not really living, and you're certainly not accepting the body you do inhabit.

Think about it. What has your "ideal" body ever done for you? Chances are the answer is nothing – because it only exists in your head! Wasting time fretting about how you look, obsessing over numbers on the scales, denying yourself the pleasure of eating biscuits are its calling cards. And all the time you've been pandering to it, you've missed out on living your life and feeling happy.

Let's change that now.

Saying hello to the body you have

You'll encounter many challenges on your journey towards body confidence. Some will come from others in the form of negative comments, some may even come from within as you wrestle with the criticisms of your inner voice. But now you're coming to the end of this section, know that you have the strength to overcome these challenges and reap the rewards that body confidence will bring.

Accepting your body, and everything you love and hate about it, is really just accepting yourself. It's about getting to know the person that resides within you, rather than focusing on what's on the outside.

You *could* choose to unequivocally hate your body. But to do that, you'll need to accept a lifetime of frustration and disappointment. And that's fine – your body, your choice. But you could choose body acceptance instead and start living your best life and all the joy that comes with it.

SEE YA, WOULDN'T WANNA BE YA

Saying goodbye is often hard – but this really shouldn't be. The "ideal" body that exists in your head is totally self-serving and undeserving of any further attention from you. So, we're going to let it go.

Jot down all the things you've missed out on because your ideal body either told you you couldn't join in, or you were so focused on trying to achieve it that you missed an opportunity. For example, staying fully clothed on a beach holiday, always offering to take family photos so you don't have to be in them, or not wearing a certain style of dress you loved for an event because you thought you were too "big" for it.

_____

_____

_____

_____

Now, list all the emotions you've wasted on it, such as anxiety, frustration, disappointment and shame.

_____

_____

_____

_____

_____

Answer this: on balance, has it been worth it? Has the relationship been a successful one?

_____

_____

_____

_____

_____

_____

And finally, are you ready to love and accept the body you're in and recognize how amazing it is? How could you do this?

_____

_____

_____

_____

_____

_____

Learning to love our body is one of the most important things we can do for ourselves. It'll sometimes be hard – some days you'll feel better about yourself than others – but it's a journey that's worth sticking with if the next time you look in the mirror, you can smile and be happy with the person smiling back at you.

PART THREE:

Love your life

Although life sometimes feels a little like running backwards on a treadmill – i.e. you feel like you're not achieving an awful lot and you're in imminent danger of falling off – most of us would agree that the good bits far outweigh the bad bits. Even if the cat's been sick on the carpet, the dinner's boiling over and you're typing a project up like some sort of multi-tasking wizard genius, you'll somehow manage to juggle it all like a pro and come out the other side feeling pretty good about it.

But if you sometimes feel like something's missing or that you're not living your life to its full potential, then it might be time to re-assess the journey you're on. In this section we'll look at the ways you can do that by improving your outlook on what you've already got and removing the obstacles that are preventing you from following the right path for you.

Satisfaction stock-check

How do you feel about your life right now? Chances are that even if you consider yourself to be living a happy and fulfilled life, there are areas you wish you felt more positively about. Perhaps you're not feeling particularly motivated at work or college right now, or maybe you're struggling for time and you've let hobbies or friendships slide. Or perhaps you're considering an entirely new path for yourself, like retraining for a change of career!

Whatever you're hoping to achieve, with a few tweaks, some new habits and a renewed sense of positivity, you can work towards finding the path that's right for you – and the best way to do this is to do a little stock-check of where you currently are.

How are you feeling about life at this moment?

_____

_____

_____

Think about how satisfied you are now and how satisfied you'd feel in five years if absolutely nothing changed. Consider what is important to you – is there a specific area of your life you want to feel better about or improve? Are there any goals you want to achieve?

_____

_____

_____

Now is your moment; make it count

KNOWING YOUR VALUES

Hopefully you're beginning to understand your own value in the world, but what do you value in your life? And what are the values that you use to define yourself?

Research suggests that our personal values contribute to the way we think, feel, act and behave, as well as help to drive, inspire and shape how we make decisions. With so much at stake, it's important we learn to know and embrace our personal values so we can be true to ourselves and live a happy and fulfilled life.

Being able to plan our lives around our values means we won't waste time and energy pursuing opportunities that might not work for us in the long run. But values also go a little deeper than that. To give our life real meaning we need to understand what beliefs and qualities are important to us.

You might already have a clear idea of what your values are – perhaps you prize loyalty, admire compassion and respect a strong work ethic – but it's also possible that you'll need a little help to work out what's important to you.

It's not something we give much thought to, it's just something we know deep inside ourselves, but analyzing what's important to us can help inform a happy future.

The doubts and anxieties you have about your own abilities are often quite useful for establishing your values. (It's about the only thing they *are* useful for!) So, give your inner critic a minute of airtime and listen to what it's telling you (then you can tell it to go away again, pronto).

If it's giving you grief over some aspect of your life or behaviour, you can use it as a signpost to where you need to focus your values.

If you feel that you've become a little lazy in your job and you're dissatisfied, perhaps you need to strive for something more challenging. Or if you're struggling to achieve your goals and your mind is telling you you're not smart enough to fulfil them, then nurturing determination and resilience will help.

What things are important to you? How might these guide your life?

Jot down your thoughts here.

What are your core values?

Circle the core values that resonate with you and add your own if you can't see it here.

Adventure

Ambition

Peace

Courage

Creativity

Dependability

Family

Friendship

Faith

Health

Generosity

Understanding

Empathy

Respect

Education

Determination

Success

Honesty

Charity

Spontaneity

Achievement

Justice

Kindness

Integrity

Intelligence

Open-mindedness

Learning

Love

Popularity

Independence

Wealth

Teamwork

Of the values you've chosen, choose the three that are most important to you. Write short, clear definitions for each one based on what they mean to you. You could even turn them into a motivating statement to use when you lose sight of a specific value. For example:

I value resilience in myself and others. I refuse to give up when I'm faced with a challenge and will always try my best to maintain my strength of mind and spirit of determination.

What habits can help you cultivate those values? Jot down your ideas here.

Boundary basics

Boundaries are rules, set by you, about how other people can treat you. Everyone has their own comfort zones, so what's OK for you might not be OK for someone else, but the principle is the same.

Boundaries are there to protect your physical as well as mental and emotional space and define the limits of your personal relationships. Setting them ensures we're taking charge of our lives and respecting ourselves, which is crucial for our well-being and self-fulfilment.

Research shows that people that set themselves healthy work-life boundaries, such as leaving or stopping work on time and prioritizing family time over work activities, are much better at managing their mental health. Conversely, research also shows that blurred boundaries, particularly between work and home life, can lead to unhealthier lifestyles and lower levels of happiness, along with a higher risk of family conflict. So, boundaries really do matter!

Setting boundaries also empowers us to know what kind of conversations we're comfortable having and how long we would stay in any situation. They let other people know your limits respectfully, without compromising the relationship.

Having your own boundaries also enables you to appreciate when and why someone else might wish to set a boundary that you'll be expected to respect.

Boundaries can also help us to develop our individuality and enable us to live in a manner that reflects our personal values and beliefs. And if we can do this, we'll find life is that bit better!

Here are some examples of expressing boundaries:

- "I don't allow people to treat me that way."

- "I don't allow people to speak to me that way."

- "Thank you for thinking of me for this project. I can't help right now, but I would love to be considered for other things in the future."

- "That's not something I want to share."

- "I'm not enjoying this. Please stop."

- "Thanks for thinking of me, but I have to say no."

- "You're standing too close. Please move back a step."

Your body is your business so only you get to decide what you will and won't do with it.

Remember, boundaries are there to give us a sense of agency in life and communicating them is essential for our health, well-being and safety.

HEALTHY BOUNDARIES vs ABSENT BOUNDARIES

Setting healthy boundaries allows you to communicate your wants and needs while simultaneously respecting the wants and needs of others. But when boundaries are absent it can lead to conflict, relationship imbalances, and often too much compromise by one party and too much control by the other.

What healthy boundaries look like...	What absent boundaries look like...
Knowing you can say "no" with confidence and respecting someone's boundary when they say "no" to you	Lacking the confidence to say "no"
Respecting different values, beliefs and opinions from your own	Disregarding someone else's request when they say "no"
Clearly communicating your wants and needs	Inability to communicate your wants and needs effectively
Having respect for yourself and your own needs, as well as the needs of others	Satisfying others by compromising on your own personal beliefs, values and opinions
Understanding social cues regarding what other people are comfortable with such as touching and personal space	Being manipulated into doing something you're not comfortable with or you don't want to do

Setting your own boundaries

If you struggle with a lack of self-confidence, it can be easy to fall into the people-pleasing trap and you might find yourself saying "yes" as your default answer to any and all requests.

But, if we can establish clear boundaries for ourselves, it makes saying "no" that bit easier, because we recognize the importance of our own needs and have the self-respect to express them confidently.

Using the core values you explored on pages 136 and 137, fill in the boxes below to discover what your boundaries are.

My core values:

1. _____
2. _____
3. _____
4. _____
5. _____

What I allow:

1. _____
2. _____
3. _____
4. _____
5. _____

What I allow but *don't* like:

1. _____
2. _____
3. _____
4. _____
5. _____

What I *don't* allow:

1. _____
2. _____
3. _____
4. _____
5. _____

Past, present, future

Thinking back and looking forward can be a positive way to look at your life: where you've been, how far you've come, what you've achieved; and also, what you're looking forward to, where you want to get to and how you might get there. It's a little like viewing your own "best bits" reel in your head and immersing yourself in all those feel-good moments to boost your mood and remember why you love your life.

Reminiscing over the past is scientifically proven to have a positive effect on our well-being. Some of these benefits include the following:

◆ Finding an enhanced purpose

◆ Discovering meaning in life

◆ Improved cognitive performance

◆ Increased self-esteem

◆ Boosted sociability

So, going on a little jaunt down memory lane is well worth the trouble!

Similarly, visualizing the future can get us closer to where we want to be in life and help us to enjoy it more when we get there. A study conducted in 2018 found that if participants took the opportunity to visualize an upcoming experience, it heightened their enjoyment of it in real time and when remembering it later. Bonus!

Immerse yourself in some time travel. What are your favourite memories? Think about what was happening and who was there.

Write about one of them in the photo frame below.

What have you got coming up that you're excited about? Write it in the crystal ball. If you haven't got anything planned just yet, use the space to plan something epic instead!

Live a life without regret

No one wants to look back on their life and regret it. Sure, we may end up regretting some of the little stumbling blocks along the way, that toxic ex-partner you wasted time and energy on, staying in an unstimulating job for way too long, studying a college course your parents wanted you to do rather than the course that you were interested in... But on the whole, we're aiming to get old and reflect on a life well lived.

The best way to live a life without regret is to consider what philosophies you want to live by. You can use the core values you've just explored (see pages 136 and 137) to inform your thoughts, such as:

I want to live with the courage to be true to myself, and not live the life that's expected of me by others.

I want to live a balanced life which includes time for family and friends, as well as work.

I want to always live within my personal boundaries and respect myself enough to call time on a relationship if my partner doesn't acknowledge this.

Starting today, how can you ensure you live a life with as few regrets as possible? What are your life philosophies?

Start practising gratitude

We've already looked at how we can practise gratitude for our bodies (see page 122), now it's time to be thankful for everything we have in life!

Gratitude has long been recognized as having proven benefits to our well-being, from helping with physical health and improving sleep quality to lifting our mood. Recognizing all the things that you're grateful for will help you to acknowledge and appreciate all the positive things in your life, even when you're faced with a challenge. Life will always contain an element of negativity (and in a way, this makes the positive bits even more worth celebrating) but studies have consistently proven that if you focus on the positive then you'll be more resilient when it comes to the negative. And, if you do experience negative emotions because of life's obstacles, science has shown that acknowledging gratitude can reduce toxic emotions.

Take the time to focus on all the things that you have. It's one of the simplest and most effective ways of improving your overall satisfaction.

Gratitude journalling

Start to cultivate an "attitude of gratitude" by spending a few moments at the end of every day writing down five to ten things you're grateful for. This could be something you've achieved, something tricky you've overcome, the affection and love of a special person or pet, doing well at work, keeping healthy, having amazing friends, and so on. Make sure you mention the small, precious moments, as well as the big-deal-type stuff!

FIND YOUR HOBBY, FIND YOUR HAPPY

Finding a hobby that we feel passionately about is like hitting the activity jackpot. Even if you suck at it, if it makes you feel good *doing* it and *experiencing* it, who cares?

If you're not convinced, here's the science: a study in art therapy showed approximately 75 per cent of participants' cortisol levels (a hormonal marker of stress) were lowered after creating art. Not only that, but the study also showed that prior experience wasn't needed to reduce stress. So that means the people who sucked at art also got the same benefits. Everyone's a winner!

But seriously, hobbies matter. And they matter because if we can carve out a little corner of the day to do something that we absolutely love, it's the ultimate act of self-care.

It could be an entirely new interest, or even something you used to do but haven't done in a while. Now's the time to get reacquainted!

What even is a hobby?

Any activity that you do for pleasure. It could be creative, athletic, academic, crafty, artistic... The sky really is the limit! All that really matters is that it's something you find meaning in. You look forward to doing it, it makes you feel alive, and you enjoy it.

You might do it on your own or with friends, outside or inside, with a team, in the community, at home, with a pet.

If you want to start a hobby but you're not sure what to try, give the fun (but completely unscientific) quiz on pages 150 to 152 a go to give you some ideas!

OK, so once I know what I want to do, how will I find the time?

Work before play makes us all a bit miserable, so it's important we make some changes to our daily or weekly routine that will free up some time so we can do the things we love.

Rather than trying to find time every day, have a dedicated "hobby day" where you throw yourself into it completely and put everything else to one side for a few hours. Schedule it in and make it a sacred day that no one can re-arrange!

There are also hidden opportunities in the day when we think we're busy but we're actually just merrily wasting time scrolling social media, looking online at holidays we can't afford or binge watching a box set, for instance.

Be mindful of how you're using your time. Can you swap some of these "autopilot" activities for hobby time?

Find the hobby for you

Try this fun quiz to get an idea of what hobby might suit your personality. Ready, set, go!

Do you prefer indoor or outdoor activities?

A) Indoor

B) Depends on the activity!

C) A bit of both, but probably more indoor

D) I'm easy. No preference

What do you want from your hobby?

A) To create something and have fun doing it

B) To do something that improves my well-being and challenges me physically

C) To do something that inspires me

D) To try something I might later pursue as a career

What do you prefer?

A) Experimenting with stuff

B) Physical activities

C) Reading a book

D) Entertaining friends

How do you want your hobby to make you feel?

A) Healthy and satisfied

B) Like I'm achieving something

C) Calm and creative

D) Like I'm centre-stage

Are you more creative than you are logical?

A) I'm a bit of both

B) Logical

C) Creative

D) Creative most of the time

What is your best quality?

A) I'm really organized and good at following instructions

B) I have physical and mental strength as well as resilience

C) People say I'm smart and bookish

D) I'm confident, full of ideas and the life and soul of the party

Do you prefer to go it alone or try something that involves others?

A) I'm happy either way

B) It depends on what the activity is

C) I prefer to be by myself

D) I want to have fun and enjoy the company of others

If you could make money from your hobby, would you leave your job and make it your career?

A) Maybe

B) No, absolutely not. It might spoil the fun!

C) It depends on other factors

D) Yes, absolutely!

How much free time do you have per day?

A) An hour or less

B) A couple of hours

C) About 3 hours

D) More than 4 hours

Mostly As: culinary whizz

Time to buy yourself a chef's hat as you'd make the ideal baker. You like to experiment, and while you're logical and can follow a recipe, you've also got a creative flair that allows you to come up with your own dishes and bakes. Your hobby will make you super popular with friends, family and colleagues as you can try new recipes out on them!

Mostly Bs: super sporty

You love the challenge of pushing your body and have probably always had an element of sportiness in your life, whether it's going for a run every day or playing in the local rugby team. You're equally happy going it alone, such as on a bike ride or swimming, or taking part in team sports such as netball or football. Gooooaaaal!

Mostly Cs: budding author

You're an inveterate storyteller and like nothing more than flexing your imagination with some creative writing. Whether it's scripts, prose, poetry or even writing your memoirs, putting pen to paper is your passion. Next stop, global bestseller lists!

Mostly Ds: a star in the making

You're fabulous on stage! Whether it's delivering a tear-jerking monologue or singing your heart out in a choir, you're destined for the stage. You enjoy working as part of a team to make a script come alive and if fame beckons then you'll grasp it with both hands. There's no stopping you!

Declutter and donate

Who doesn't love a good declutter? Not only is it great for getting us doing something productive that will (hopefully) enhance our living space and therefore our lives, but it's also good for clearing some mental headspace too.

This is because living in a messy or cluttered living space is often an extension of what's going on inside our heads. If we're living among a mess, we're telling ourselves that it's OK for our lives to be a bit of a mess too. The negative impact of this is that you'll feel less in control of your environment.

You need to show yourself that you can manage challenges by mastering the mess! If you're facing a mess-mountain the size of Everest, just tackle one small area at a time so you don't feel too overwhelmed.

The excellent news is that all that clutter might do some good. If you've chucked out some bits you don't need but the items are still of a good quality, why not donate them to a charity or shelter? Not only might it benefit someone else, but it'll also give you a warm sense of well-being that'll boost your mood.

So, if you're holding on to a mystery set of keys that ought to be in the bin or you've got an excess of clothes that don't fit and need a new home, it sounds like it's time to declutter your house and headspace!

Love your friends, love your family, love your life

Lots of things make us happy, but science has proven that having good friends makes us our happiest. Hurrah!

In one of the longest-running scientific studies into happiness, the data shows that relationships are the number one key indicator of joy and happiness. The study by the Harvard Study of Adult Development began in 1939 and involved over 700 male participants from which data was collected over the next 80 years – so they've got a real handle on what makes us happy.

The scientists wanted to know what experiences in earlier life predicted health and well-being in later life. And the results were conclusive, yet also surprisingly simple: the only factor they could correlate with happiness was the quality of the human relationships the participants had formed over their lifetimes. Close friendships, family connections, marriages and partnerships surpassed other variables like social class, genetics, intelligence, fame or fortune. The participants who were most satisfied in their friendships at the age of 50 were the healthiest and happiest at age 80.

So, there you go – having an amazing set of friends and a strong family unit really does make you happier. If we can cultivate and hopefully maintain even just a handful of close relationships, it could have a direct impact on our happiness and sense of fulfilment later in life.

Good friends are like gold dust...

Now we know just how important our friendships are, how can we make sure we're nurturing them so they can withstand the test of time, and roll with all those life-punches? After all, we need good friends when we're down as well as when we're up. In fact, it's at those times that we often need them even more.

Here are the six secrets of a good friendship:

1. **Support.** Friends are the bedrock of our support system but don't forget that support is a mutual pact you enter into when you become friends with someone. Friendships are built on reciprocity: help them out when they need it and they'll be sure to help you too.

2. **Absolute mutual trust.** If you can't be straight with each other or are keeping things hidden then you're on shaky ground. Relationships need a solid foundation and lies and untruths erode this. It'll come toppling down the next time there's a crisis.

3. **No judgement.** You might be joined at the hip and share a similar outlook on life but, if a friend makes a choice you don't agree with (unless it puts them in imminent danger), it's your job to support and accept their choice rather than judge them. Their life is still theirs and yours is still yours.

4. **Respecting boundaries.** Respect their comfort zones and they will respect yours, whether it's talking about a past trauma or being ashamed of something they've done. Be honest with each other but also mindful of any lines that shouldn't be crossed.

5. **Total kindness.** Don't criticize or bad-mouth a friend behind their back.

6. **Forgiveness.** We all screw up and no one is perfect. Be willing to accept and forgive each other's mistakes and it'll be much more likely that the relationship will last.

LIFE GOALS

Daily life can be overwhelming at the best of times. Even mundane tasks, such as getting the kids to school on time, ordering the food shop, dealing with bills, and checking up on a vulnerable loved one, can conspire to ensure we spend every day feeling like we're treading water and not really achieving anything.

The problem with this is that sometimes we might have a life goal that we want to accomplish – big (planning for a career change, moving to the countryside) or a little smaller (trying a new hobby, learning a new subject) – and it might require a change of direction. In turn, this often prompts our voice of self-doubt to pipe up saying things like "You'll never see that through", "You haven't got time for that", or "You'll definitely fail". This voice can make us want to either procrastinate or give up before we've even started!

But what if you break the goal down into smaller, more achievable, steps? Not only will the goal seem a lot less daunting, but every time you tick off another completed step it'll give you a mini confidence boost that'll encourage you to keep going.

Think of a goal you're working towards. It can be anything: home improvements, a project at work, finishing a craft project, getting on top of life admin, tidying a cupboard, and so on.

You might only have one, or you might have several! Jot them down here.

Break it down

Make sure each step is **S**pecific (so you know when you've achieved it), **M**easured (how you will know when it's done), **A**ttainable (so it can feasibly be achieved), **R**ealistic (so it doesn't feel too overwhelming), and **T**ime-bound (so it can be completed within the time frame you've given yourself).

SMART

For example, "I want to sort out my vintage record collection. I'll donate the ones I don't want to a second-hand record shop and put the ones I'm keeping in alphabetical order on the shelf. I only want to keep 50 of my favourite records. I want to do it by the end of the month."

Pre-planning

What has inspired me to do this?

_____

Who will I be accountable to?

_____

Are there any obstacles that could stop me?

_____

Task	Planning	Started	Almost done	Finished	My reward
_____	☐	☐	☐	☐	_____
_____	☐	☐	☐	☐	_____
_____	☐	☐	☐	☐	_____
_____	☐	☐	☐	☐	_____
_____	☐	☐	☐	☐	_____
_____	☐	☐	☐	☐	_____
_____	☐	☐	☐	☐	_____
_____	☐	☐	☐	☐	_____

Reflect and regroup

I found the following hard _____

I found the following easy _____

I really enjoyed _____

I got a lot of satisfaction from _____

I learned _____

I'm inspired to _____

KEEP YOUR FOCUS

You're now the proud owner of a set of goals – go you! Not only that, but you also know how you're going to achieve them. But how will you stay focused on them when you're faced with lots of distractions?

Some of these may be unavoidable, but things like spending half an hour looking at cute kitten memes on social media can spell disaster for keeping our minds on the prize. In fact, in one 2017 study into smartphone usage it was found that the average person checks their smartphone 47 times a day. That's almost six times an hour in the average 8-hour working day!

While smartphones, social media and surfing the internet account for some of the external distractions we're likely to face, it's also possible that you'll distract yourself from achieving your goals because of your inner mindset.

Whether you're prone to listening to your voice of self-doubt or you're the master of procrastination, here are some tips for keeping your focus and staying on the path to glorious goal-dom:

◆　Always make sure your goals align to your core values.

◆　Be open to reviewing your goals and accepting changes you need to take to achieve them.

◆　Find someone who is willing to be your "accountability partner" – someone who can help you reach your goal because they'll hold you to your word.

◆　Focus on the outcome. You've got this!

IF YOU'RE FACING IN THE RIGHT DIRECTION, ALL YOU NEED TO DO IS KEEP WALKING

FIVE FABULOUS WAYS TO WELL-BEING

Research undertaken by the UK's New Economics Foundation has found that long-term well-being is achievable for all of us if we can incorporate five key actions into our daily lives.

Sounds simple, and it is! Try to include as many of the activities suggested below as you can and it'll help you get the most out of your life.

Stay connected

Maintaining strong relationships with the people in your life is not only an important form of support, but having close connections to family, friends, colleagues and your community is crucial for your sense of self-worth and belonging. Try to catch up with someone you care about every day. You don't need a reason, just get in touch!

Take notice

Being aware of the present moment and the environment around you can enhance your well-being and reaffirm your life priorities. It also allows us time to be introspective, which helps us understand ourselves better.

Never stop learning

Continuing your learning journey past your school years will enhance your self-esteem and encourage social interaction. It's also a great confidence booster! You could try something new or reignite an old hobby.

Stay active

Thirty minutes a day is all you need to boost your physical and mental well-being. It doesn't have to be intensive to count – just walking to the shops or pottering about in the garden will make you feel better.

Give to others

Get a warm fuzzy feeling by giving regularly, whether that's your time, your charity, supportive words or a kind gesture. Helping in your local community is a brilliant way to get the feel-good factor, and you'll be enhancing the lives of other people too.

Fill in the table below with how you could incorporate the five ways to well-being into your life.

Stay connected	*e.g. schedule family time.*
Take notice	*e.g. start the day with 10 minutes of mindfulness.*
Never stop learning	*e.g. sign up for a new course.*
Stay active	*e.g. go for a lunchtime walk.*
Give to others	*e.g. help a friend out.*

Learning for life

When was the last time you learned something new? Science tells us that learning new skills can literally reshape our brain. This means that not only does learning provide us with an opportunity to concentrate and increase our focus, but it helps to root us in the moment and calm down our thinking brain (the one that's constantly firing to get us through the day). It also reduces stress, create new connections in our brain and makes us feel happier. And, perhaps most importantly, we get to master a new skill to show off!

You don't have to dive straight in and try learning advanced mechanics or philosophy – unless you want to, of course – but taking some small, achievable steps towards broadening your knowledge can never be a bad thing. You don't need to become an expert, just give it a go and enjoy the process.

30-day learning challenge

1. Read an article about an unfamiliar subject
2. Listen to a podcast
3. Attend a public lecture or talk
4. Learn an unfamiliar word and its meaning
5. Watch a TED talk about a subject that interests you
6. Learn a handful of phrases in another language
7. Learn a dance move
8. Sign up for a trivia night or pub quiz
9. Read a chapter of a book
10. Learn how to repair something
11. Visit a museum, heritage site or art gallery
12. Watch a debate
13. Learn about another country and its culture
14. Practise meditation
15. Buy a crossword, puzzle or sudoku book and complete one a day
16. Learn an art technique
17. Teach someone else something you recently learned
18. Practise mindfulness
19. Sign up for an online course
20. Read about a world view that is different to yours
21. Take part in an online Q & A
22. Test your knowledge on a subject
23. Learn a new physical skill
24. Listen to an audio book
25. Learn about local wildlife, and look for the creature or insect next time you're on a walk
26. Do a still life drawing of something special to you
27. Learn a productivity technique
28. Teach yourself a new recipe and cook it for a loved one
29. Learn a fact about what happened on this day 100 years ago
30. Learn a poem that touches you

Boost yourself back up

What brings you to life if you're having a bit of a "meh" day? We've all got a special something or someone we turn to if we need a life lift. While that thing is different for everyone, they've all got something in common – they give us the feel-good factor when we most need it.

Anything that re-energizes us counts, whether it's listening to some hype music, meeting up with a friend who always makes us laugh, taking some time out to just sit quietly with our thoughts, or doing something active that gets our heart beating a little quicker.

MY ENERGY BOOSTERS

Fill in the space below with a list of all the things, people and actions that give you all the good feels. You could add words, names, mantras, drawings... anything you like! Next time you need a boost, you'll know where to look!

Next time I want to turn my "meh" day into a marvellous day, I will...

Put your life under the microscope

Another way we can help ourselves live our best lives is to look at the patterns of "meh" and "marvellous" over the course of a week to see if we can spot any patterns and work out if we can rejig our time.

Take time out at the end of each day to reflect on when you felt at your best. Jot down some brief notes about each day, including what made you feel fabulous and what made you feel a bit flat.

Mon	Tue	Wed	Thur

Fri	Sat	Sun

Your inner child

A study found that our childhood experiences can teach us life lessons that help us adapt to situations across our entire lifespans – so those formative developmental years really do shape the adults we become. Although we think we've forgotten the things we experienced at, say, age five, science shows that we can tap into those lessons much later in life. This means that being in touch with the inner child that still resides within us could be beneficial to us as adults.

Grown-ups tend to be quite rigid in their thinking, but children tend to be open to new ideas. They see the possibilities in everything in a way that adults don't, so it makes sense that if we switch ourselves to "child mode" we'll become more open to the opportunities that exist all around us. And through a sense of wonder and curiosity, often comes a sense of joy.

Try the following ideas to help you connect with your inner child and regain a sense of wonder:

◆ Browse the old family photo albums to bring back memories of your childhood.

◆ Make time to do what you enjoy.

◆ Be playful and engage in creative play, such as colouring or making an obstacle course.

◆ Make sure there's laughter in your life.

◆ Write a letter to your inner child (see pages 124 and 125).

◆ Journal about any special memories from your childhood.

◆ Engage in meditation and creative visualization to help you engage with your inner child.

THE POWER OF NATURE

Nature is such a gift at any time of year, whether it's crunching through some frosty autumn leaves, watching your garden come to life in spring, or embracing whatever the winter or summer brings.

The sense of wellness we get from immersing ourselves in nature is hard to beat. Even if it's windy, rainy or just generally gloomy outside, getting in touch with the natural world has been scientifically proven to increase feelings of positivity. In fact, just 20 minutes in nature can lower our stress hormones and give us a dose of mood-boosting Vitamin D from sunlight.

If you can, try to incorporate regular time in nature into your weekly schedule to really maximize the benefits it can give. If you have a local green space, woods, coastal or river walk (where you'll get the additional benefits that being close to water brings, such as a sense of calmness), get out and get exploring!

If you can't go far, or you've got limited time, you could try gardening or growing house plants. If you've got a family, rope the kids in to help and they'll be benefitting too.

Top mood-boosting activities outside include the following:

- Visiting a nature reserve
- Playing with a pet in the garden
- Stargazing
- Beachcombing or volunteering for a beach clean-up
- Picnicking in your favourite spot
- Cloud watching

If getting outside is tricky, why not bring nature in? Here are some top mood-boosting activities to do inside:

- Create a nature nook by the window where you can watch wildlife and the changing seasons.

- Buy flower seeds and make a pot display on your windowsill or invest in some houseplants that you can nurture and watch grow.

- Create a nature sounds playlist and use it as a soundtrack to visualize an outdoor adventure.

- Immerse yourself in a nature video.

- Start your own herb nursery.

- Fill your walls with your favourite nature pictures. You could even make your own artwork or collage and reap the well-being benefits of doing something creative.

Up your green credentials

There has never been a better time to be more mindful of our global impact on the planet. Not only do we have a collective responsibility to live in an eco-friendlier way but being "green" with our life choices can also give us purpose and a self-worth boost as we'll know we're doing something for the common good. It'll also help safeguard all the natural spaces and habitats, as well as the creatures that call them home, for us and for future generations. After all, if we want to love our lives, we need a planet to live them on.

Here are some ways you can reduce your environmental impact:

- Repair items wherever possible instead of buying replacements
- Start a compost heap
- Recycle everything you can from your rubbish
- Walk, cycle, use the train or bus, or carpool places
- Buy local produce
- Have 5-minute showers
- Turn off the tap when brushing your teeth
- Reuse and refill containers and cups
- Have a clothes swap with similar-sized friends
- Donate to eco-causes
- Help with community litter picking or beach clean-ups
- Unplug gadgets that aren't being used

There is
never a better
moment than
right now

Set your intentions

What would your life look like if all the stars were aligned? Sometimes it can feel like we're drifting through life and just letting it "happen" to us rather than being an active participant. If we set intentions for ourselves on a daily, weekly, monthly or even yearly basis, we can make sure we're living with purpose and making progress towards a life that's authentic and aligned to our values.

Intentions are an expression of our determination to do something. It's different to goal setting because it isn't a plan that you see through to completion – it's more of a behaviour or practice that you want to manifest in your daily life.

When we set an intention, we are making a commitment to ourselves and making ourselves accountable to act towards achieving our vision. They can help us focus on short-term results, such as achieving tasks on our to-do lists, as well as helping us to envision how we want to feel while we action them. For example:

Today my intention is to focus on finishing my project, and I'll approach it with determination and joy.

By expressing your intention, you're giving yourself a better chance of succeeding because you're stating explicitly how your vision will become a reality – which will keep it at the forefront of your thoughts. In the longer term, we can use intentions to steer our lives in the direction we want to go and help us stay on track when things get challenging.

Practise writing some of your daily, weekly, monthly or yearly intentions below.

_____

_____

_____

_____

_____

_____

_____

_____

_____

_____

_____

_____

_____

_____

My vision board

Things you need:

- **A large piece of card or paper**
- **Pen**
- **Colouring pencils**
- **Photos (optional)**
- **Glue (optional)**

Your intention could affect momentous change in your life, such as moving to a new area or getting a new job, or it could be something smaller you wish to accomplish by the end of the day. Whatever your intention, know that having a vision of it can help to guide you in the direction you want to go.

Create a vision board to help bring your dreams to life. Write and sketch the images and words that best represent what you're aiming for on a large piece of paper. For example, if you want to change career, write down some of the words associated with that field, what it might be like at a new job, what you'll be doing and how it makes you feel. You could even stick photos around your words and drawings that represent your journey and your vision for the future.

When you're done, hang your board somewhere you can see every day. Remember to look at your vision board as often as you can to remind you of your dreams. You could even use your vision board during mindfulness or visualization practices.

Use your board to inspire you and help you to set your intention. Remember to try to keep it clear and concise and dream as big as you want!

Find your inspiration

"The pen is mightier than the sword," wrote Victorian author Edward Bulwer-Lytton, and this is certainly true when it comes to the power of inspirational quotes.

Whether they've originally been said out loud and instantly resonated with you, or you've read something profound in a book, or heard something in a film that made you laugh so much you cried, we've all got a handful of quotes that bring a smile to our face when we think of them or empower us if we're feeling a bit deflated. Quotes allow us to ponder, question and consider, and appreciate wisdom from figures past and present.

Write your favourite inspirational quotes alongside any new ones you hear in a notebook. Refer to them whenever you need a laugh, a boost or a general reminder that life is good. Use words to inspire wellness and positivity rather than trying to fight fear with aggression or avoidance.

Habits... and how to break bad ones

Habits just happen. We spend a lot of our day on autopilot, and habits often take care of all the mundane stuff that we don't have the headspace to give much thought to. So, we do them without question – especially the bad ones, like having five sugars in our morning coffee or checking our phone notifications every time one flashes on screen.

Sometimes they serve a purpose and can be quite helpful in terms of living your life, such as always starting your day by making goals and setting intentions on a whiteboard or having a routine that you stick to so you can get everyone out of the house on time.

But because we don't stop to question how helpful our habits are where we just do them out of routine, there's a good chance you've picked up a few bad habits along the line that have seamlessly snuck into your life without you even realizing.

From a scientific perspective, it's all to do with feeling safe. When you act out a habit, the feel-good hormone dopamine is released in your body and you get a little boost of happiness. That's why your daily morning coffee tastes so good, or that much-needed glass of wine at the end of the week is so sweet.

But while some habits might feel good, they may not actually be beneficial for you.

Let's tackle those unhealthy ones first...

Breaking bad habits

This may require a little resilience and willpower, but it's worth it if it means you'll no longer be bound to your bad habits.

If you're committed to making the change, consider the following:

♦ Does your habit have a trigger? Stress, anxiety, feeling low, being around certain people, low self-esteem, being hangry, the time of day, and so on all can make us want to reach for the comfort blanket our habit provides. For example, if you're wasting a lunch hour on social media, is it out of boredom? Or escapism?

♦ Try to avoid the things that enable you to engage in your bad habit. Put that phone away and fill your time with a healthier habit, such as going for a walk.

♦ Become more mindful of your actions and thoughts. Do you really need to reach for your phone, or is it just an avoidance strategy because you need to start writing an important document and you don't know where to start?

Habits... and how to develop good ones

Just as bad habits can bring negativity to our lives, healthy habits can have a positive impact and enable us to develop positive values. Studies have suggested that the likelihood of maintaining a good habit increases substantially after 18 days, so if you can stick with the programme, you've got a good chance of the healthy habit becoming a permanent fixture.

It doesn't need to be hard to establish a new, healthy habit, just follow these simple rules:

◆ Make sure your environment is conducive to making the change. For example, if you're swapping snacking on chocolate bars for a piece of fruit or a handful of nuts, put the chocolate away and set the fruit bowl centre-stage on the kitchen table.

◆ Start small and regularly remind yourself of why you're making the change. Remember the benefits and use them to motivate yourself.

◆ Link new habits to existing healthy habits. For example, if you want to form a de-stressing habit, tag a 10-minute meditation onto your usual bedtime routine.

◆ Congratulate yourself mentally when you execute your habit effectively. This'll help your mind build a positive association, and you can use that feeling of achievement to spur you on next time.

Healthy habits, happy you

Write down the unhealthy habits you'd like to break and any healthy habits you'd like to start doing more of in your life.

Unhealthy habits	Healthy habits

THE WORLD IS BIGGER THAN ME

You can give meaning to your life by joining a cause you feel passionately about. Happiness – and the pursuit of it – is an integral part of being human, but to ensure your life means something you need to go beyond your own wants and needs and partake in activities that reflect something that's bigger than yourself and your own small world.

> Happiness is an emotion, which means it can be felt in the moment and then fade away, but meaning endures beyond the present moment – it connects the present to both the past and the future.

It's about finding a purpose – creating goals that not only benefit you but could potentially benefit others too.

Being able to engage with things outside of ourselves, such as supporting a non-profit social justice organization, affecting change in your local community, campaigning for a cause that reflects your values and beliefs or regularly volunteering at the local refuge centre are all activities that give shape and meaning to our existence.

See your contribution to something bigger as your legacy – not just to yourself and those around you, but to the world.

Don't panic; prioritize

How do you make sure you maximize every day? It's all too easy to get bogged down with the minutiae of everyday life and sometimes it feels like we're adding more tasks to our weekly to-do list than we're accomplishing. Little wonder we start to feel overwhelmed and then, inevitably, we start to question whether we're any good at adulting after all.

When we're faced with a list of tasks and it's making us break out in a cold sweat because of the sheer length of it, prioritization tends to go out of the window, and we find ourselves just muddling through regardless of what should be done first or what is most important.

Evaluate the urgency of tasks using a time matrix (see pages 186 and 187) and allow yourself to prioritize the things that bring you happiness. When we put our well-being at the top of our to-do lists, we maximize the amazingness of our lives.

MY TO-DO LIST

Use the space below to offload all the tasks in your head.

You could just write the tasks for today or note ones for the entire week. It doesn't matter if it's boring or small, such as booking a food delivery slot or organizing your day bag – if it's in your head, write it down!

_____

_____

_____

_____

_____

_____

_____

_____

_____

_____

_____

_____

_____

_____

The time matrix

Using your list from pages 184 and 185, write down your activities and responsibilities for the week in the relevant quadrants on the following page, evaluating how urgent and important each one is.

Separating out tasks visually like this helps us to clearly see that not everything we think we need to accomplish every day is what we actually need to do. If it's urgent and important – do it! But if it's neither of these, either park it until you've done everything else or forget it completely.

Use the matrix to prioritize whenever you're feeling overwhelmed. It's based on productivity guru Stephen Covey's "Time Management Matrix", and it'll simplify your life as well as freeing you up so you can spend more time doing the things you love.

	Urgent	**Not urgent**
Important	Do:	Delay:
Not important	Delegate:	Dump:

THE END

Now you've finished this book, it's time for you to find your own way to being amazing – and you absolutely will. Whether you've been inspired to make some instant changes in your life or you need a little more time to get your thoughts together before you take the leap, know that there is no right or wrong path to feeling amazing – just take the one you know feels right for you.

You've already done the hard bit by picking up this book, reading it to the end and hopefully having tried some of the activities too, and that's amazing! If now isn't the right time, this book will be here waiting for you when it is.

How you choose to perceive your mind, body and life is up to you, but if you choose to pursue genuine happiness in all three areas, you'll see just how amazing you can be.

FURTHER READING

If you need any further support or information, the following will also help you on your journey towards wellness.

Books

Find Your Why (2021), Joanne Mallon

Love Your Life: 100 Ways to Start Living the Life You Deserve (2021), Domonique Bertolucci

Podcasts

Go Love Yourself – An empowering podcast hosted by Laura Adlington and Lauren Smith exploring body confidence, diet culture, social media and mental health. Weekly episodes.

Ten Percent Happier with Dan Harris – Dan looks at the best ways to bring happiness into your life. New episodes three times a week.

The Art of Being Well – Dr Will Cole explores ways in which you can nurture your body, spirit, mind and relationships, and use self-care to enhance your self-respect.

Wellness with Ella – Ella and her guests reveal their personal journeys of growth and provide inspiration to transform your life. Weekly episodes.

Websites

Happify – www.happify.com

Life Hack – www.lifehack.org

TED's Positive Playlists – www.ted.com/playlists/673/10_days_of_positive_thinking

The Body Positive – www.thebodypositive.org

YES YOU CAN
Hardback
ISBN: 978-1-78685-979-2

JUST BE YOU
Hardback
ISBN: 978-1-80007-184-1

NEVER GIVE UP
Hardback
ISBN: 978-1-78685-978-5

**THINK POSITIVE,
STAY POSITIVE**
Hardback
ISBN: 978-1-80007-701-0

HOW TO BE BODY CONFIDENT

A Toolkit to Help
You Transform Your
Relationship with Yourself

Olivia Roberts

Paperback
ISBN: 978-1-83799-027-6

Love and accept yourself just as you are

There are so many things to celebrate about your body. Just think of everything it's got you through – the happy times and the challenges – and all the wonderful things it enables you to do each day. Sometimes, it's important to be reminded that your body is uniquely yours, and that's what makes it so special.

This guided journal is here to help you shed body shame for good, so that you can feel confident in yourself every day. By engaging with the tips and activities inside, you'll learn how to see your body in a different light, quit negative self-talk and start speaking to yourself with love and kindness.

Have you enjoyed this book?

If so, why not write a review on your favourite website?

If you're interested in finding out more about our books, find us on Facebook at Summersdale Publishers, on Twitter at @Summersdale and on Instagram and TikTok at @summersdalebooks and get in touch. We'd love to hear from you!

Thanks very much for buying this Summersdale book.

www.summersdale.com

IMAGE CREDITS